SOUTHAMPTON
MURDER VICTIMS VOL 2

SOUTHAMPTON
MURDER VICTIMS VOL 2

JIM BROWN

First published in Great Britain in 2012 by The Derby Books Publishing Company Limited, 3 The Parker Centre, Derby, DE21 4SZ.

This paperback edition published in Great Britain in 2013 by DB Publishing, an imprint of JMD Media Ltd

ISBN 978-1-78091-085-7

Printed and bound in the UK by Copytech (UK) Ltd Peterborough

CONTENTS

ACKNOWLEDGEMENTS

I am deeply indebted to the following, without whose assistance this book would not have been possible (unattributed photographs and illustrations are from my personal collection):

David Hollingsworth, Vicky Green and the staff of the Local Studies Section, Southampton Reference Library, whose extensive archives of local newspapers provide so much valuable material for researchers; Sue Woolgar (City Archivist) and the ever-helpful staff of the Southampton Record Office, whose archives, again, are absolutely invaluable; Nina Fairbrother (Southampton Bereavement Services), who spent much time and effort providing me with precise grave locations in all the Council cemeteries; John and Gillian Dunkason (Friends of Southampton Old Cemetery), whose expertise in locating burial plots in the Old Cemetery revealed otherwise untraceable memorials; likewise Phil Chandler, Eastleigh Cemeteries and Open Spaces Officer; Mr Keith Wiseman, (HM Coroner), Howard Willis and Phillip Harris, (Coroner's Officers), for access to restricted Coroner's material; Paul Stickler, Peter Stoddard, Derek Stevens and Dr Clifford Williams, BA, M.Phil, PhD (Hampshire Constabulary History Society); Karen Manners, Assistant Chief Constable of Warwickshire & West Mercia and former Head of Hampshire Constabulary Serious Crime Directorate; Mark Gould, Dave Hambrook MBE and Mark Sansbury, (Hampshire Constabulary Archives) for facilitating my unrestricted access to files held by the Hampshire Constabulary; Aaron Brown, Hampshire Constabulary Publications Officer; Lucy Dibden and Hayley Court, Hampshire Constabulary Media Services Dept.; Dave Goddard, for generously providing photographs of long-vanished public houses from his vast collection; and to Ian Abrahams, Bitterne Local History Society; Alison Potten and Natalie Johnson, Southampton City Council; Denise Hoy, Jenny Singleton, Janet Holloway and Ian Murray, Editor, *Southern Daily Echo*, for allowing me to reproduce their photographs.

Last, and by no means least, my wife Marion, who proof read my drafts and patiently accepted my prolonged absences in the archives and in my study firmly attached to my keyboard, as well as accompanying me on my searches through local churchyards.

The book is dedicated to Paul Stickler, ex-Chief Superintendent responsible for policing the City of Southampton and Chairman of Hampshire Constabulary History Society, for his enthusiasm, dedication and outright hard work, without which this book would not have been contemplated.

Paul was unfortunately struck down by a serious illness a matter of weeks before the book was completed and thus unable to complete a planned Foreword. Fortunately, his involvement was taken over by Chief Inspector Clifford Williams, who not only completed reading drafts, suggesting amendments and corrections, but also greatly assisted in obtaining further source material. For this work Paul and I are truly grateful.

Jim Brown
July 2012

FOREWORD

I am very pleased to have the opportunity to write a foreword for Jim Brown's *Southampton Murder Victims Volume 2*.

It makes a change to read a crime book that gives more prominence to the victims than those who committed the crime. The inclusion of memorials with photographs of graves in some of the cases adds to the emphasis on the victim perspective of these murder cases.

This book, like Jim's excellent *Southampton Murder Victims* (2010), presents material in a factual and contextual way. While there is no playing down of the horrendous nature of these crimes, Jim has been careful not to reproduce sensational and gory material. As one reviewer of his 2010 book put it, 'the book is sensitive without being mawkish.'

Southampton Murder Victims dealt with a wide range of cases from 1783–2009. In this book the majority of murders were committed in the last 20 years. While the forensic tools now available to the police have greatly assisted success in detection of these crimes, the demands of the criminal justice processes have become more cumbersome. Much police work now goes into 'homicide prevention' by 'managing' dangerous offenders and working with other agencies to try and safeguard potential victims. This is demanding work given the number of potentially violent offenders who are living outside the security of prison walls.

In 1952 Jim joined Southampton County Borough Police (as it was then called) as PC 150 James William Maxton Brown. His personal insight into police work, as well as his detailed knowledge of the city of Southampton, makes this book an authoritative addition to our knowledge of the darker side of the city's history.

This book has been produced with the assistance of the Hampshire Constabulary History Society. The Chairman of the Society, Paul Stickler, and others, including myself, have been pleased to help Jim collate material from sources held in the Constabulary archives and not generally available to the public.

Clifford Williams BA, M.Phil, PhD
Chief Inspector

INTRODUCTION

This book is a sequel to *Southampton Murder Victims,* produced in 2010 by DB Publishing and the present book is a joint publication with DB Publishing and the Hampshire Constabulary History Society. The former book explained, in some depth, the various amendments to the original mandatory death penalty for murder; the stages of penal servitude that were imposed, until abolished in 1948; an explanation of the former Assize Court system, and the establishment of the Crown Courts that replaced them in 1972.

My available sources were also explained, i.e. a list of persons committed to the Hampshire Assize Court at Winchester 1876-1942 found in the city archives; the Inquest Registers held by HM Coroner giving basic information, with dates of unlawful killings (a Register known of and made available to me as a former Deputy Coroner's Officer); together with archive murder material held by the Hampshire Constabulary History Society, the comprehensive records held by the Local Studies section in the Southampton Reference Library and the Southampton Record Office in the Civic Centre. Further source material was also found at the National Archives, Kew.

I was fortunate, with the assistance of the current local Coroner's Officers, to be given unrestricted access by HM Coroner to inquest files held by the Southampton Record Office. This gave me additional useful information that helped me to accurately complete the present accounts of individual murders.

I also had assistance, as in the previous book, from the Southampton Bereavement Services and Friends of Southampton Old Cemetery, who, between them, enabled me to locate and take photographs of many graves of unfortunate victims. Some of those not recorded locally were found by searching the graveyards of local churches, but others were untraceable.

The archive murder material already held by the Hampshire Constabulary History Society had been enormously enlarged by the personal help of senior members of the police service and history society. This allowed the transfer of scenes of crime photographs and other material held in police archives to the history society archives, giving the present book many examples of previously unpublished material.

Unfortunately, because of differing storage locations and differing recording systems over the decades, plus the need to remove records because of limited space, especially where cases have been dealt with and the sentences served, many files are no longer available. However, the police archive staff went to great lengths to search through their 16,000 large boxes of archive material to locate as many as possible for me.

Other photographs were obtained through the Hampshire Constabulary Media Department, who supplied them strictly within the restrictions imposed by legislation and the Association of Chief Police Officers Communication Advisory Group Guidance 2010.

For all the above I am extremely grateful.

Human rights legislation, the Rehabilitation of Offenders Act 1974 and the Data Protection Act 1998 can all inhibit factual accounts of incidents involving offenders who are still alive. Because the Rehabilitation of Offenders Act considers a sentence of 30 months or less to be 'spent' after 10 years, I have had to take this on board. In such cases I have called the killer their Christian name to conform to the requirements of the Act. This normally applies to convictions for manslaughter, as opposed to those of murder.

Fortunately, much of what I have written is already in the public domain via the detailed and accurate reporting of trials in the excellent local newspaper, the *Southern Daily Echo*, and the national press.

I have, however, although taking external photographs of murder scenes from the public highway, made efforts to restrict information by removing vehicle registration numbers and house numbers. I have also abided by the code of practice involving the naming or identification of juveniles, unless made available by the court.

I trust that the reader will find my accounts of interest and very much hope they go some way to perpetuate the memory of those unfortunate victims, whose lives were cut short and their human rights removed by the actions of others.

Jim Brown
July 2012

At the New Scotland Yard Detective Training School in 1960.
(**Author standing third from right in the front row.**)

1873 – DANIEL BROWN – THROWN OVERBOARD

Francis Shephard, 34, a seaman, said to be 'of imperfect education', appeared before the Hampshire Assizes on 15 July 1873 indicted for 'the wilful murder of Daniel Brown in the roadstead of St Vincent on 11 April last'.

The circumstances were that on that date the ship, the *T and G* of Gloucester, was at anchor off Cape St Vincent, Portugal, and Shephard, Brown and two other seamen had permission to go ashore. At about five o'clock the captain and four other crew went to fetch them in a dinghy and found they were all on the beach, drunk. Shephard managed to get into the dinghy but the other three had to be carried there, they were so drunk.

Shephard and Brown then began to quarrel, Shephard saying that Brown ought to be ashamed of himself for being a Scotchman and letting himself get so drunk. Brown started shouting and Shephard then said 'If you don't be quiet I'll heave you out of the boat'. As the quarrel continued, and intensified, Shephard took hold of Brown's arm and leg and threw him overboard.

The water was three fathoms deep at this point and a seaman, called Toulman, called out that Brown could not swim. The men could see Brown at the bottom, in the clear water, kicking, but were unable to do anything to save him. They had no option but to return to the ship without Brown, who had by then clearly drowned.

The captain's son, Archibald Rees, who was only an apprentice, witnessed everything and later made a deposition to the consul at St Vincent, as did the captain and other crew members. Shephard was detained on board until the ship arrived at Southampton, when he was handed over, with the depositions, to the Southampton police at the Bargate, who charged Shephard with murder.

Both Toulman and Rees gave evidence at the Assize Court, with the depositions accepted under the Merchant Shipping Act. At the conclusion of the prosecution case the judge said he could not see that it was a case of murder, 'the throwing of a sailor overboard in sight of land, not being that kind of act which in the ordinary course of events must necessarily cause death'. The defending counsel, Mr Matthews, invited the jury to consider that Brown, when in a helpless state of drunkenness, attempted to rise to his feet when Shephard touched him and he fell overboard.

The jury could not agree and 'were then locked up', and on their return found the prisoner 'not guilty'. The judge then expressed the hope to Shephard that what had happened would be a warning to him for the rest of his days, and discharged him.

1873 – HANS BJERRITZ – KILLED OVER A CABIN DISPUTE

The 2,000 tons British steamship SS *Olbers* left Buenos Aires, South America, on 9 March 1873, bound for Southampton carrying cargo, passengers and mail. Among the 190 passengers were Matthew Keogh, 41, an Irish shoemaker travelling with his wife, and Hans Jurgen Bjerritz, from Denmark.

Earlier, when the ship left Rio de Janeiro, the ship's steward, John Brown, discovered that the extra passengers who boarded there meant he had to rearrange some cabin allocations. In the course of this he placed the Dane, Hans Bjerritz, into a cabin with four other passengers. Bjerritz had violently objected to this, saying, 'Why did you not change that ——— Irishman's cabin instead of me?', indicating Matthew Keogh and his wife, but the steward said he could not now alter things.

During the afternoon of 21 March, while the ship was at sea, Bjerritz was sitting on deck, holding a heavy piece of wooden batten, about four feet long, four inches wide and an inch and a half thick. Matthew Keogh and his wife walked past him and as they did so Bjerritz got up and tried to hit them with the batten, swinging it from left to right. Mrs Keogh pushed her husband out of the way and Bjerritz stumbled, recovered and made a second attempt to strike Mr Keogh, but again missed.

Keogh, who had been drinking heavily, suddenly took a knife from his left hand pocket, shook it open, lunging at Bjerritz as he swung around, and struck him in the back. The knife was a Spanish spring one, a foot long , that opened when shaken. Bjerritz staggered away, saying as he did so 'Oh God, oh God, I'm stabbed' and fell to the deck. Keogh then drew the knife across his trousers, as though to clean it, closed it and replaced it in his pocket, but his wife took it out, presumably to ensure her husband could not use it again.

Dr John Walsh, the ship's surgeon, was sent for and found Bjerritz lying on the aft hatch. He examined him and found a puncture wound between the ninth and tenth rib, about four inches from his spine. Bjerritz was taken to a cabin where he died from an internal haemorrhage at half past seven that evening. A later examination showed that the wound was five inches deep.

George Tanner, the ship's officer, took the knife from Mrs Keogh and detained her husband, whereupon Mrs Keogh fainted. When the ship arrived at Southampton the ship's master, Captain Harby, informed Southampton County Borough Police who attended and arrested Matthew Keogh. He was taken to the town police station at the ancient Bargate and later charged with murder.

Keogh appeared at Hampshire Assizes, Winchester, on 15 July 1873 and pleaded 'not guilty'. Several witnesses testified that the deceased was 'an ill-tempered man' with a

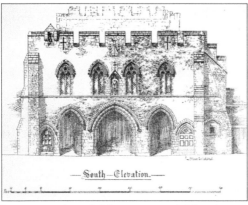

—South—Elevation.—

A 19th-century view of the south side of The Bargate. The small left hand door led directly to the police station.

history of violence on board, and that Keogh was clearly drunk at the time of the stabbing.

Mr Bullen, for the defence, put forward a case that there was no evidence that the SS *Olbers* was a British ship, as her registration had not been proved, and this was essential for the case to be dealt with by a British court. The ship's officer, George Tanner, was then recalled and he stated that the vessel was owned by Messrs Lambert of Liverpool. This proved sufficient for the judge to allow the case to proceed.

Mr Bullen then tried to persuade the jury that any offence committed by Keogh was manslaughter, not murder, because he was defending himself from a further attack and

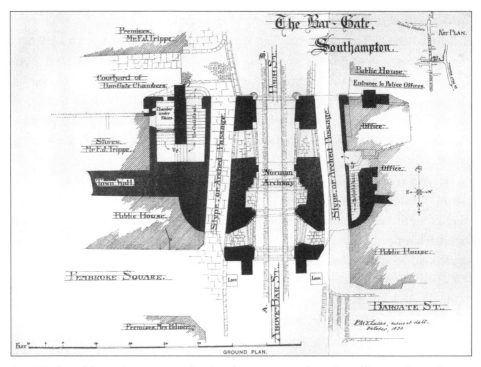

GROUND PLAN.

An 1833 plan of the ancient Bargate, showing the entrance to the police offices on the south-west corner, with stairs leading direct to the upper Guildhall, where Magistrates Courts were held and prisoners committed to the Winchester Assizes.

was also heavily under the influence of alcohol. He also said, 'I regret that I am unable to call the prisoner's wife, but the law does not allow me to do so. She would have put before the jury clearer evidence than any other person and the whole truth of the transaction.'

The jury retired and then returned with a verdict of 'guilty of manslaughter'. The judge then said 'it was as bad a case of manslaughter as one could possibly imagine. No doubt the prisoner had received provocation but it was such that it could have been overcome.' He then added that in sentencing he would rather err upon the side of mercy than of severity. 'The term to which I am about to sentence you will conduct you from middle to old age, and it is that you be kept in penal servitude for twenty years.' Mrs Keogh was then carried out of the court 'in violent hysterics' by two policemen.

The 1881 census shows Matthew Keogh as an inmate in HM Prison, Princetown, Dartmoor, but his ultimate fate is unknown. One must assume that on his eventual release he returned to his native Ireland.

1885 – EMILY COOKE – A SHIRLEY TRAGEDY

An inquest took place at the Shirley Hotel, on the corner with Park Road, on the evening of Thursday 19 March 1885, before Mr Bernard Harefield, deputy county coroner, into the deaths of John Pelham Cooke, 67, and his wife Emily Cooke, 40, at 32 Regent Street, Shirley. Both had been found dead the previous day at their home, which also served as a general shop.

The Shirley Hotel (left, on corner of Park Street) as it was in this period. (*Dave Goddard*)

After the jury was sworn in, and a brief explanation of the procedure given to them, they all adjourned to 32 Regent Street to view the bodies, which were lying separately and not coffined! They saw the mark of a blow, the size of a crown piece, on Mrs Cooke's forehead.

On their return to the Shirley Hotel the first witness, who also lived in Regent Street, at No.46, was Mrs Maria Broomfield, Mrs Cooke's sister. She said that Mr Cooke was well known as the former landlord of the Blue Boar and Horse & Groom public houses, both in East Street. The couple, she said, lived very unhappily together as he had a dreadful temper. She didn't know why he treated her sister so unkindly, with such abusive language, and 18 months ago he had threatened to take her life. Emily, who was much younger than him, was his second wife; the first had died some years ago.

Mrs Broomfield last saw her sister at nine o'clock the previous Tuesday morning, 17 March and her husband at two o'clock that afternoon. Both appeared to be their normal selves. At seven o'clock the following morning the milkman called at her house, as she lived opposite her sister, to say there was a note on the door saying 'This shop will be closed for a few days' and he couldn't make anyone hear.

Mrs Broomfield also tried the door and then became concerned, deciding to call at the police station in Shirley Road. Detective Hunt of the Southampton Police was Mrs Cooke's brother and he was sent for and later attended.

PC Edward Brown, of the Hants Constabulary stationed at Shirley (Shirley was not incorporated into Southampton Borough until 1895), gave evidence that he took a ladder to the rear of the house and gained entry by breaking an upstairs window. He found John Cooke downstairs, sitting in an armchair, 'very pallid, warm and seemingly only just dead'.

He had let Sgt George White into the house, and he gave evidence of finding two empty bottles alongside Mr Cooke, one of them labelled 'laudanum', a small quantity of which was in a nearby empty beer glass.

Beside it was a portrait of Cooke's first wife. There was also a thin rope tied around his neck. A poker was found in the grate close by Mr Cooke, but there were no marks on it.

Emily Cooke was found at the bottom of the stairs, lying on her side, clearly dead, with some rigor mortis and an obvious blow to her head, which was lying in a pool of blood. There were also splashes of blood on the passage wall and on her apron. A thin piece of rope was tied very tight around her neck, with a knot. All the doors and windows of the house were securely locked and the premises secure with no sign of a forced entry, other than the window broken by PC Brown.

There were initial concerns for the Cooke's five-year-old son, but he was traced to the home of Mrs Sarah Rowe, confectioner, in Shirley High Street. John Cooke had taken

Redcar Street, on the corner with Shirley High Street. Formerly Regent Street, until renamed in 1903. (*Dave Goddard*)

him there at nine o'clock the previous evening, wrapped in a shawl which was later found to show traces of blood. He seemed very excited and in a hurry and asked her to take care of his son as his wife was very ill. He also gave her a note which read:

'March 17th Dear Friend, I, having appointed you executor of my will and guardian of my son, I wish you to take possession of my house and property as soon as possible. Yours truly, John Pelham Cooke.'

The son was seen by the sergeant but all he could say was that he had said his prayers to his father before he went to bed.

Dr Caesar, of Shirley, deposed that he had examined the bodies in Regent Street and John Cooke had not died through taking laudanum but by strangulation. The cord around his neck had been wound around and twisted twice, the first coil being tighter than the second. His wife had sustained a wound on her forehead that extended down to the bone, but, again, death was due to strangulation. The wound was caused by something knobbed, like the poker found at the scene. He formed the view, from examining the scene (one of the early scenes of crime officers?) that Mrs Cooke was passing from the shop to the living room when she was struck on the head and that after falling to the ground she was strangled with the cord. From the state of the bodies it was certain that Mrs Cooke had been killed some considerable time before her husband died, at least 12 hours, and in view of the blood on the boy's shawl, that this had been carried out before he was taken to Mrs Sarah Rowe's home.

The coroner spoke to the jury at length on the fact that their duty was to find the causes of death and how it was brought about. There was no evidence as to the man's state of mind but as far as it went it seemed to show sanity rather than insanity.

The jury then retired for a private consultation for a quarter of an hour, returning to announce that Emily Cooke was murdered by her husband by strangulation and that he afterwards took his own life, he being in a sound state of mind.

Emily Cooke is buried in Shirley churchyard and John Cooke in Southampton Old Cemetery, with his first wife, in plot C015 169.

The site of Emily Cooke's grave can no longer be seen as the area was grassed over, to form a recreation area in the churchyard. The memorial stones were removed and placed along the route of an adjoining path.

The memorial stone, however, can still be seen, although worn. It reads:

> IN MEMORY OF
>
> EMILY COOKE,
>
> WHO DIED MARCH 17 1885
>
> AGED 40 YEARS.
>
> IN THE MIDST OF LIFE WE ARE IN DEATH.
>
> ALSO
>
> ANN HUNT,
>
> MOTHER OF THE ABOVE
>
> WHO DIED NOV 12 1893

John Cooke's grave is alongside a path in Southampton Old Cemetery and the headstone reads:

> IN AFFECTIONATE REMEMBRANCE OF ELIZA,
>
> THE BELOVED WIFE OF
>
> JOHN PELHAM COOKE,
>
> WHO DIED DECEMBER 5TH 1875 AGED 43 YEARS.
>
> 'AFFLICTION SORE LONG TIME SHE BORE
>
> PHYSICIANS SKILL WAS VAIN
>
> TILL DEATH DID SEIZE AND
>
> GOD DID PLEASE
>
> TO EASE HER FROM HER PAIN.
>
> ALSO OF
>
> JOHN PELHAM COOKE
>
> WHO DIED MARCH 18TH 1885
>
> AGED 62 YEARS.

1900 – JOHN DWYER – THROWN DOWN THE HATCH

On 25 January 1900 the steamer SS *Rustington,* owned by Messrs Ball, Symonson & Co., of Fenchurch Street, London, sailed from Barry Docks, Wales, bound for Santos, Brazil, with a cargo of coal from Cardiff. Among the crew were two Able Seamen, George Francis McGough, 27 and John Dwyer, 39.

George McGough, born in Duncannon, Ireland, lived at 15 St George Street, leading from Lower Canal Walk, Southampton, and was described as a 'diminutive but powerfully built Irishman'. Welshman John Dwyer kept a Seamen's Boarding House, with his wife Mary, in Thompson Street, Barry Docks and had seven children, the eldest being 20 years old.

On 10 March, while the ship was docked in Santos Harbour, both men went ashore, returning between 9pm and 10pm. George McGough was drunk, reeling and belligerent, saying 'I want to fight somebody'. Four other crew members, Walter Greeley, Johan Lundberg, George Burton and Gustave Nillson, saw John Dwyer try to persuade McGough to go below but Dwyer was then struck in the stomach, picked up bodily and thrown down the forehatch, a distance of 26 feet.

Dwyer fell headlong into the hold, striking his head on timbers below as he landed, and was seen to immediately steadily haemorrhage from his mouth and both ears. When crew members went down to see what they could do they found he had died within minutes. McGough was detained by the captain and handed over to the British Consul in Santos, while John Dwyer was buried ashore.

The Consul handed McGough over to the captain of the Royal Mail ship *Magdalena,* to be taken to Southampton, the ship's home port, and arranged for the four witnesses (named above), who were the *Rustington*'s ship's carpenter, bosun and two deckhands, to be also taken to Southampton by the first available British steamer.

When the *Magdalena* arrived at Southampton Det.Sgt Edgar Tribe went aboard, arrested, cautioned and later charged McGough with murder and he replied, 'I have done it like a man and I will suffer for it like a man'.

He appeared before Mr Justice Lawrence at the Winchester Assizes on Monday 2 July 1900, and pleaded not guilty. After hearing the evidence of the crew members, the judge instructed the jury that 'there is no case of murder made out, even though it is a precept of the law

George Francis McGough. (*Hugh McGough*)

that a person can be presumed to intend the probable and natural consequences of their actions'. The jury then returned a verdict of guilty of manslaughter and McGough was sentenced to 15 months imprisonment with hard labour.

There is a twist to the story.
McGough was an active member of the Seamen's Union and returned to sea on his release from Winchester Prison (he is shown in the prison on the 1901 Census). McGough represented the Union on the 'Lifeboats Subcommittee' of the Board of Trade, whose 1911 recommendations were shelved, and married a Southampton woman, Beatrice Nellie Gannaway, who was 10 years his junior, in 1912.

The marriage took place just before he sailed as deck crew on the ill-fated RMS *Titanic* on 12 April 1912. George helped to load and lower lifeboats on the stricken ship's port side, before crossing over to the starboard side, where he was saved by leaving in Lifeboat Number Nine.

The twist to the story is that another Southampton convicted murderer was also on board RMS *Titanic*, William Mintrim. His story is told in the author's prequel, *Southampton Murder Victims*, but unlike George McGough, he did not survive, having passed his lifejacket to his son-in-law, Walter Hurst.

1921 – LILLIAN WHEELER – A LOVER SPURNED

Lillian May Wheeler, known as Lily, aged 19, was the eldest of her family and lived and worked at the Blue Bell Inn, Briton Street, Northam. She was engaged to John Alexander Thomas, generally known as Alexander or Alex, aged 25, the youngest of his family, with whom she had been 'going steady' for the previous three and a half years. They had known one another all their lives and both had attended the local Northam School. It was their intention to get married at Christmas, 1921.

The Blue Bell Inn, 23 Briton Street, on the corner of Charlotte Street. (*Dave Goddard*)

The public house has long since vanished, with the site now occupied by a massive block of apartments. The area was extensively developed during the post-war construction of the Queensway Inner Ring Road.

Briton Street ran from Orchard Place to Lower Canal Walk and was in the working class area of the lower town. It is known, for example, that the nearby small house opposite, No.10 Briton Street, was occupied by five families, a total of 18 individuals all living in rented rooms, including the cellar.

John Alexander Thomas had led a troubled life. When he was nine years old he had suffered a heavy fall, causing severe concussion of the brain, and throughout his life he frequently complained of pains in his head.

However, this did not prevent him joining the 5th Battalion the Royal Hampshire Regiment when he was 18 years old and serving in the 1914-18 war.

During his army service he spent three years in India, where he contracted malaria, from which he never fully recovered. On his return to Southampton after the war he spent three months in the Royal South Hants Infirmary suffering from this fever.

John Alexander Thomas, 'Alex', photographed in India during 1914-18, with his pith helmet on the floor alongside. (*Denise Hoy – Alex's great niece*)

Following his recovery he obtained work as a boilermaker with the ship repairers Day, Summers and Co., ship and yacht builders, but he was 'stood off' when he finished his time. He then completed several trips on the liner *Imperator* (purchased by Cunard in April 1921 and re-named *Berengaria*), with his last trip in November 1920, but he was then unable to obtain further work. He remained unemployed for almost a year, until obtaining a final voyage on the *Berengaria*, returning to Southampton on 28 October 1921. It was said that the long period of unemployment, coupled with little prospect of getting further work, worried him and gave rise to periods of depression.

Alex lived at 3 Southampton Place, Back-of-the-Walls, with his brother George, who later stated that Alex had been so depressed that although they were good friends he would sometimes pass George in the street without speaking.

Lily was normally a cheerful girl and everybody knew that she and Alex were very much in love. However, the path of true love does not always run smooth and on the evening of Saturday 5 November 1921 the couple had a quarrel, severe enough for her to tell him their engagement was over. The cause of the disagreement is not known, but

RMS *Berengaria*, named after the consort of Richard the Lionheart.

Lily's mother, Mrs Ellen Kettle, heard Alex ask Lily to 'make it up', but she refused, saying she wanted nothing more to do with him.

On Sunday afternoon the licensee of the Blue Bell Inn, Walter Wells, was repairing a metal coil in the workshop of 10 Briton Street when Alex entered, carrying a German rifle. He asked Mr Wells to clean it for him, in exchange for Alex carrying out the repair to the coil, and this was done. Mr Wells asked if the rifle was a wartime souvenir, but Alex did not reply.

The next day, at 1.35pm Monday 7 November, Mrs Florence Wells, the wife of the Blue Bell licensee, went across to the wash-house at the rear of 10 Briton Street, where she saw Lily. Lily said she had quarrelled with Alex, who wanted to make it up, but she had no intention of doing so. Mrs Wells then turned round and saw Alex, 'his eyes ablaze', pointing a rifle over Florence's shoulder towards Lily. She shouted, 'Don't shoot, Alex' but he fired simultaneously with her pushing the gun up in the air. She did not look round to see if Lily had been hit but ran out, frightened, across to the Blue Bell, where she told her husband what had happened.

Walter immediately went across to No.10, where he saw Alex stretched out in the yard 'with his head practically blown off and the German rifle between his legs'. Lily was on the floor of the wash-house with a bullet wound in her forehead.

Police Constable George Offer attended the scene and found a cartridge case in the breech of the rifle and another on the ground. The bullet that killed Alex could not be found but the one that killed Lily was found on the floor. It was a 'dum-dum' (a small arms bullet with a soft nose, designed to expand upon contact and cause a gaping wound).

From the nature of Alex's wounds it appeared he had placed the barrel of the rifle in his mouth and then fired. As the three feet six inches long rifle was breech-loading, with no magazine, he would have had to reload it before turning it on himself.

The constable found two live cartridges, one of which was also a 'dum-dum', in Alex's pocket. He also found an engagement ring in Lily's pocket, suggesting she had told Alex that the engagement was off. This could have triggered off his attack. The constable stated that the wash-house, around 6 x 12 feet in size, had a large copper in one corner and a sink in another. There was also a large mangle, covered in blood, as was the wall behind it.

At the inquest, held on Thursday 10 November, the coroner pointed out to the jury that if they found Thomas was not of sound mind at the time their verdict need not be that a crime had been committed. The jury, without retiring, then gave a verdict that Thomas shot Miss Wheeler and himself while of temporarily unsound mind.

John Alexander Thomas and Lillian Wheeler. (published in the *Southampton Times*)

John Alexander Thomas is buried in Southampton Old Cemetery, in unmarked plot D184/264 and Lillian Wheeler in Hollybrook Cemetery, in unmarked plot M/007/52.

1925 – ARTHUR HEYWOOD CLEWS – A GALLANT CAPTAIN

Arthur Heywood Clews, 49, born Birkenhead, often boasted that he was the only Clews that ever went to sea. Leaving school at the age of 14 he was apprenticed to the New Zealand Shipping Company and over the years served as second officer, first officer and then captain on cargo ships under sail. In 1904 he changed from sail to steam, joining the Canadian Pacific Railway Company as fourth officer when they first entered the Atlantic trade.

On 23 January 1905 while Arthur was serving as third officer on the TSS *Monteagle*, a seaman fell overboard in Barry Docks and without hesitation he plunged into the icy water and supported the man until he was saved. For this he was awarded the Royal Humane Society diploma for saving life.

Captain Arthur Clews. (*Southern Daily Echo*)

At the outbreak of World War One he was sent to the Cameroons and promoted to take command of a German prison ship, which he sailed to England. His appointment as captain was then confirmed and he took command of several ships, on several occasions acting as Commodore of convoys. During the war he made 15 voyages to Canada in command of troopships and post-war resumed command of a number of Canadian Pacific vessels, the last being the SS *Melita*.

The SS *Melita*.

Among the officers on board in October 1925, under Capt. Clews' command, were Thomas Augustine Towers, 56, from Bristol, First Officer; David Gilmour, 42, from Glasgow, Second Engineer; and John Holiday, 41, from Bootle, Junior Second Engineer.

Thomas Towers had yet to take command of a ship. He had earlier been appointed to take command of one but this had been cancelled after only 10 days because the ship was being laid up. For some reason Towers blamed Captain Clews for the failed promotion and this came to light on board the *Melita* at Southampton on 17 October when Towers had an argument with another officer, Sidney Allen.

Towers had accused Allen of complaining to passengers about the captain's behaviour and also writing to the company office about it, but this was strongly denied. Matters came to a head between the two and Captain Clews became aware of it and called them into his cabin, where they were joined by other officers. All were asked if they had seen Allen talking to passengers, and when they all said 'No', Captain Clews said to Towers, 'Now Towers, I know it is not Allen, you will be surprised what I know'.

SOUTHAMPTON MURDER VICTIMS VOL 2   25

Although unconfirmed, it is suspected the captain believed that it was Towers who had complained to passengers and written to head office, attempting to deflect this away from himself by accusing Allen.

Whatever the reason, Towers later told other crew members that he was the victim of a conspiracy among the officers and that they had formed a plot against him. It was noticed that Towers would frequently stay in his cabin for 12 or 14 hours at a time.

On the evening of 20 October 1925, while the ship was berthed at Antwerp and due to return to Southampton the following day, Towers went ashore, returning at 2.30am. He spoke to the third officer, Mr McClellan, about more fresh water being needed and at that time appeared perfectly normal, speaking in a friendly manner.

However, at 3.30am he woke David Gilmour, the Second Engineer, who was sleeping in his cabin, and complained, in a bullying manner, that the ship was listing badly to starboard. Gilmour replied that Towers should have stayed on board to look after the ship, refused to take any action himself, and went back to sleep.

A short time later he was suddenly woken by the shock of a bullet fired into his face, and glimpsed Towers standing over him with a revolver in his hand. The bullet had entered through Gilmour's nose and settled behind his ear. John Holiday, Junior Second Engineer, then entered the cabin, having heard the shot, and saw Gilmour in his bunk, badly injured and bleeding heavily from the wound in his face. He saw Towers standing there and said, 'What have you done?', but Towers replied, 'Stand back or you will be hit'. Holiday then rushed at Towers, who immediately shot him in the chest, the bullet penetrating a lung. Other officers then rushed into the cabin and grappled with Towers, striking him in the face and wrestling the revolver from his hand. He was then handed over to the ship's Master-at-Arms, Mr Elliott, who had also arrived at the scene.

Towers then said, 'I have shot the captain', and that was the first that anyone knew of this. The ship's doctor, Dr James Benny, was sent for and went at once to the captain's cabin and found him dead in his bunk. He was lying on his right side, with some blood on the pillow, and a wound in his left eye that appeared to have penetrated the brain. He had been dead for about an hour. The doctor formed the opinion that the captain had been shot while asleep.

The Master-at-Arms was told and, after handcuffing Towers, cautioned him and charged him with the murder of Captain Clews. Towers replied 'I intended to shoot the commander, Gilmour, Allen, McCellan, the purser and myself, only the gun failed'.

Both injured engineers were taken to the local hospital, where bullets were removed from Holiday's lung and Gilmour's head, both officers making a full recovery. When the ship berthed at Southampton the following day it was boarded by Detective Chief Inspector Dan Lucey and Inspector William Parker. They saw the captain's body, which had not been disturbed, and also checked Towers' cabin, where they found a pistol magazine with five live cartridges in it, together with 12 others in a drawer. Thomas Towers was then taken to the Bargate police station and charged with the murder of Arthur Clews and attempted murder of the two engineers.

Thomas Towers appeared before Mr Justice Rowlatt at the Hampshire Assizes, Winchester, on 18 November 1925, when there was some initial discussion as to Towers' fitness to plead and 'so bereft of understanding that he could not be tried'. The prison doctor, Dr Thomas Richards, said he had had the prisoner under his observation since 22 October and found he was suffering from delusional melancholia but showed no symptoms of insanity. After a brief deliberation the jury found Towers fit to plead and he then pleaded 'not guilty' to all three charges.

After all the witnesses had given evidence the jury retired and returned after 20 minutes, finding Towers guilty of all three charges. The judge then sentenced Towers to be detained in Broadmoor Hospital 'until His Majesty's pleasure be known'. The local newspaper the following day came out, predictably, with the headline 'Towers guilty but insane'.

Captain Arthur Clews is buried in Bebington Cemetery, Birkenhead.

1925 – ROY HYAMS – UNFIT TO PLEAD

Sarah Hyams, 31, was led into the dock at Winchester Assizes, before Mr Justice Rowlatt, on the morning of Saturday 14 November 1925, supported by two prison wardresses. She was sobbing hysterically and had to be supported as she leant against the dock rail. The charge against her was that on 3 September that year she had murdered her six month old baby son, Roy, by drowning him in the bath at 28 East Park Terrace, the home of her husband's parents.

Sarah had then placed the unfortunate child's body in a suitcase, travelled by the

5.40am newspaper train from Waterloo and threw the suitcase onto the railway line from the moving train at Brockenhurst. When it burst open, revealing the baby's body, it was found by a signal linesman, Mr Gill.

East Park Terrace. (*Eric Gadd*) The entire terrace was demolished post-1945 and the site developed.

Brockenhurst Railway Station.
(*John Fairman*)

The body was dressed in new clothes that were soaking wet, and he appeared well nourished. The police were called and as a result of labels and other details found on the suitcase, the baby was identified by his grandfather, Mr Hyams, of 28 East Park Terrace. As a direct result of what he told the police, his daughter-in-law was arrested at Boscombe, in a distressed state, a few days later, and admitted what she had done.

Enquiries revealed that although she was very intelligent, with a BA degree, she had been very demented since the boy's birth and obsessed with the idea that he had rickets, had a broken spine and was deaf. In fact, the child was perfectly healthy. The distraught Sarah was therefore charged with murder.

She was not represented at the Assizes and the prosecuting counsel, Mr Escott Williams, asked the judge's permission to put to the jury that Sarah was unfit to plead. His Lordship told the jury that the question for them was, therefore, not was she mad at the time she killed the boy but was she so mad now that she could not be tried?

Dr Richards, the medical officer at Winchester Prison, said the prisoner was suffering from 'a bad form of mental melancholia'. He, when questioned, confirmed that Sarah would not understand an oath, was incapable of intelligently following the proceedings of the trial and was incapable of defending herself or instructing counsel on her behalf. He also stated, when asked by the judge, that she could not follow a trial or take in what was said to her.

The hearing had only lasted four minutes and Sarah, who was still crying loudly, was assisted from the dock as the judge ordered her to be 'kept in strict custody until His Majesty's pleasure be known'. Baby Roy is buried in the Hebrew section of Southampton Old Cemetery, in unmarked grave E32-207.

1935 – GEORGE ROWE – A BRUTAL HAMMERING

The headlines of the *Southern Daily Echo* on Wednesday 29 May 1935 were eye-catching: 'SHOLING STAGGERED BY SHOCKING DOMESTIC TRAGEDY – DEMENTED MAN ATTACKS HIS WIFE AND CHILDREN – Attempt to hammer them to death – Garden shed turned into a shambles'.

As the story unfolded it revealed that shortly after 10 o'clock that morning screams were heard and Mrs Caroline Dyer, 34, was seen rushing out from her home in Butts Road. She ran into her next door neighbour's house, with blood streaming from her head, shouting, 'Come quickly, help me to save my children, he has got them in the shed.'

Screams were heard coming from the garden shed at the back of Mrs Dyer's house, and her neighbour, Mrs Annie Kilford ran to it but was unable to open the shed door. At the same time Harry Burden, a window cleaner working nearby, arrived on the scene after hearing the screams, and also attempted to open the shed door. It was resisted from the inside but after a struggle he managed to force it open and found it had been held back by Mrs Dyer's husband, Thomas Dyer, 40, an unemployed rigger.

Thomas was drenched in blood and rushed towards Harry Burden, kicking him in the stomach and dropping a hammer from his hand as he did so. Harry then punched Thomas in the jaw, knocking him to the ground.

Inside the shed were three children, all suffering from head injuries and covered in blood. They were Frederick Dyer, aged 6; Iris Dyer, aged 4; and George Rowe, aged 3, a nephew, who was lying on the floor, underneath a bicycle, with blood pouring from a terrible wound in his head. The two Dyer children were cowering in the corner, screaming in terror. They were all removed by Harry Burden and his workmate, Mr Mattingly, who had followed him into the rear garden.

Thomas Dyer then got up and was held by Mr Burden and Mr Mattingly, who then saw that Thomas had a gaping wound in his throat and was semi-conscious.

Two ambulances arrived at the scene (operated by the fire department at this pre-NHS period) having been called by neighbours, and PCs Padwick and Blowes arrived in one of them. Mrs Dyer and the children were taken to the Royal South Hants Hospital

The Royal South Hants Hospital, as it was in 1935.

The Dyer and Rowe home in Butts Road.

in one ambulance, where surgeons battled to save the children's lives. However, Thomas Dyer, who was taken in the second ambulance, with the police officers, died during the journey.

The *Echo* reporter wrote 'When I arrived less than half an hour after the occurrence I saw a pathetic little figure standing forlornly at the door of the Dyer home. His eyes were filled with tears and he was inconsolable. He was nine years old Tommy Dyer, the eldest of the Dyer's three children. When his father seized the other three children he also attempted to push Tommy into the shed, but Tommy, luckily for him, eluded his father, ran as hard as he could from the house and hid in some bushes in an adjoining field. Kindly neighbours were endeavouring to coax Tommy away from his tragic home but they could not prevail upon him to leave.

While I was talking to him another pathetic figure came stumbling down Butts Road, half-fainting and pushing a pram, in which was a baby only a few months old. She was Mrs Maude Rowe, the mother of George Rowe, the most critically injured of the children. She and her husband, Mr George Rowe, rented two rooms at the house, with their two children and she is the sister of Mrs Dyer.'

The reporter later interviewed Mrs Dyer, who said, 'Tom told me at breakfast he was going to mend one of the children's boots. When I was washing up the breakfast things I told him that if he started the mending job I would get the children tidy so that when the boots were finished they could all go out. Tom went out to the shed to get the hammer he uses for boot mending. When he came back I was putting the crockery on the dresser when he came up behind me and hit me on the head with the hammer. Then he dashed into a cupboard, I suppose he got the razor then, I think I must have collapsed.'

The situation changed at 11.30am the following day when the unfortunate little George Rowe died from shock, multiple depressed fractures of the skull and loss of blood. He had eight wounds to his head.

When the inquest on both George Rowe and Thomas Dyer opened on 31 May 1935, Harry Dyer, brother of Thomas Dyer, said he last saw his brother, whose general health was poor, on 27 May. He had suffered from gastric ulcers for two years and had been unemployed for about seven months. Thomas had become worse in mind and body a week before the tragedy and had become morose. However, Harry Dyer said his brother had always been a good husband and a good father, kind and devoted to his children. The Dyers had been married for 10 years, the whole time spent in the house in Butts Road. The inquest was adjourned as Mrs Caroline Dyer was too ill to give evidence and the condition of her two children was still very poor. The inquest was then adjourned to 2.30pm Thursday 27 June 1935.

Mrs Dyer, dressed in black, gave evidence that day, saying that her children were still in hospital but slowly recovering. She said that her husband had seemed very depressed about a fortnight before the incident and she had sent for Dr Dunlop when Thomas became very strange in his manner. The doctor advised that he should rest and to send for him if he became worse.

Describing the events of 29 May, she said the family had breakfast at 7.30am, after her husband had spent a restless night, wandering about the bedroom. After breakfast she asked him how he felt and he said he was better, although she could see he was trembling. At about 10am he came into the kitchen, without saying anything, and then suddenly hit her on the head with the hammer, without warning. She managed to turn and run out of the house and shortly afterwards heard children screaming in the shed. She was asked if her husband had ever had 'these semi-brain storms' before or threatened suicide, and she said he had not.

The jury returned a verdict that Thomas had murdered George Rowe and committed suicide while of unsound mind. Thomas is buried in unmarked grave 152-71 and George Rowe in unmarked grave H23-373, both in St Mary's Extra Cemetery, not too far from their home.

1936 – JAMES BURNS – A SHIPMATE'S FATAL QUARREL

The Cunard White Star liner *Berengaria* left Southampton for New York on 2 December 1936 and first called at the port of Cherbourg. On board were two shipmates, James Burns, 35, from Bridgeton, Glasgow and Charles Edward Ridgeway, 34, of Taunton, Somerset. The two seamen

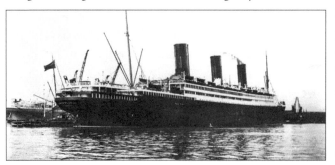

had been shipmates on a previous voyage, when they had shared a cabin, but this time they each had their own quarters.

The *Berengaria* at Southampton in 1924.

Shortly before noon, while the ship was moored in Cherbourg, Ridgeway, who had been drinking heavily, was dozing in his bunk when Burns entered the cabin and demanded a drink. He was also drunk and in an aggressive mood. Ridgeway told him that he had nothing to drink, whereupon Burns immediately butted him in the mouth with his head. Although Ridgeway was a tall and powerful man, he did not retaliate but left the cabin.

He was seen with his mouth bleeding by the Master-at-Arms at 3.30pm that day, who asked what had happened. Ridgeway said he had again been assaulted by Burns, who had once more demanded a drink. Ridgeway said this time he had been thrown to the deck, rolling along with Burns on top, trying to strangle him. He had, however, managed to get away.

The ship left Cherbourg at 8.30pm that evening, by which time the two seamen had been drinking almost continuously throughout the day. Shortly afterwards Ridgeway was seen passing along an alleyway going towards Burns' cabin. Five minutes later a seaman named Brading heard two heavy thuds outside his cabin and on going into the alleyway saw Burns holding a knife with the point facing out aggressively. He was staggering along the passage with blood pouring from a wound in his neck, muttering to himself. He only went a further six paces when he collapsed. Burns did not get up and when he was examined by the ship's doctor was found to be dead. A later post-mortem carried out on board confirmed that Burns had died from a massive haemorrhage as a result of the main artery in his neck being partially severed.

The captain was informed of the situation and he interviewed members of the crew. A boy seaman had seen Ridgeway coming up the companionway, from the direction of Burns' cabin, with his hands covered in blood. He told the boy he had cut his hand on a hatch and when the boy offered to go for the ship's doctor he was told that the doctor had already been seen. This was not true. No one else was able to give any direct account of what had happened to Burns in his cabin.

Ridgeway was also seen and made a long statement, admitting having fought with Burns and describing the quarrels with him over drink during the day. The statement ended with his account of going to Burns' cabin, where Burns asked him to shake hands. He had declined and as he turned round, Burns jumped on top of him, trying to slash at his face with a large kitchen knife.

He stated, 'I raised my left arm to protect my face and received the knife on my arm. He had me tight up against the door and I was almost powerless. I tried to take the knife from Burns and nearly got it, but managed to push Burns away from me. He staggered and fell. I left Burns in his room. I did not know if or not he was injured, things happened so quickly. If I did stab him, I do not remember doing it, it was my life

Det.Insp Percy Chatfield. (*Southern Daily Echo*)

I was fighting for. I was back to the wall, unarmed, face to face with a man who was mad drunk and I was a lucky man to get out of the room alive.'

The captain took possession of a large pantry knife found with Burns' body and a sheath knife found on the floor of the washroom where Ridgeway had been seen bathing a wound in his left forearm. When the ship returned to Southampton on Wednesday 16 December, 1936, he gave them to Det.Insp. Percy Chatfield, together with statements made by Ridgeway and other crew members. Det.Insp. Chatfield then saw Ridgeway, who was detained in the ship's isolation hospital, cautioned him and told him he was going to take him to the Civic Centre police station. Ridgeway said 'What is the exact charge?' and told that if a charge arose he would be told later.

At the police station Ridgeway was shown the sheath knife but denied it was his. He also denied taking the large kitchen knife from the pantry, saying it must have been taken by Burns. He tapped the statement he had made to the captain and said, 'I know before God and man that it is wrong to injure another. All I have to say is in that statement.' Det.Insp. Chatfield later charged Ridgeway with the murder of James Burns and he replied, 'I plead not guilty to the charge'.

The cell passage in the Civic Centre police station, together with an interior view of a cell. This is one of the 17 male cells into which Ridgeway would have been placed after arrest. Southampton County Borough Police moved into these newly constructed Police Headquarters in November 1933.

At the subsequent committal proceedings before Southampton Magistrates on 19 January 1937, there was a good deal of discussion as to where any trial would take place.

Mr Hughes, solicitor for the prosecution, pointed out that the bulk of the witnesses were crew of the *Berengaria* and any seaman kept on shore to give evidence was entitled to full maintenance and wages. This would be paid from funds provided by Parliament. The Winchester Assizes were more than a month away but the *Berengaria* would be laid up from 10 February to 24 February, so witnesses would then be available and not lose work. The Central Criminal Court (The Old Bailey) was available on 9 February, the day before the *Berengaria* was laid up, so the prosecution asked the bench to commit the accused there for trial.

However, Mr Emanuel, solicitor for the defence, said that a country solicitor could not be expected to know London barristers and suggested either Exeter or Bodwin Assizes, both of which were on the Western Circuit. After much deliberation the magistrates decided to commit the accused for trial at Exeter Assizes, which were to open on 16 February.

Ridgeway thus appeared before Mr Justice MacNaghten at Exeter Assizes on that date and pleaded 'not guilty'. The two knives were the principal exhibits in the case. The large pantry knife that disappeared from the kitchen on the night of the alleged stabbing was only seen in the possession of the deceased, James Burns. The sheath knife found on the floor of the washroom, the prosecution suggested, could have been the weapon that killed Burns and used by Ridgeway to self-inflict the wound on his arm.

Both knives were bloodstained and Dr John Thomas, police pathologist, said the blood on the sheath knife was insufficient to group. From Burns' bloodstained clothing he deduced that he was group OMN and that was the same group on the large kitchen knife. A few spots of blood on the lapel of Ridgeway's coat were group A.

The judge, in his summing up, told the jury that apart from the statement of the accused, there was no direct evidence as to what happened when Burns received the wounds from which he died. He said, 'It is circumstantial evidence and I direct that it is not sufficient that the circumstances are consistent with the guilt of the accused. In some cases it is open to you to return a verdict, not of murder but of manslaughter. No such alternative verdict can arise in the present case'.

Unsurprisingly, the jury, after an absence of three quarters of an hour, returned a verdict of 'not guilty' and Ridgway was discharged. On hearing the verdict Ridgeway almost collapsed with shock and had to be helped from the court by police officers to join his waiting friends.

1937 – AMELIA LINDEN-HITCHCOCK – A TRAGIC DISCOVERY

In 1937 PC William McShane, Shirley Division, was a close friend of the Linden-Hitchcock family who lived at 235 Millbrook Road (a small villa that was swept away in the post-war reconstruction of the A33 dual carriageway).

Thomas Linden-Hitchcock.
(*Southern Daily Echo*)

Thomas James Linden-Hitchcock, 60, an unemployed bricklayer, lived there with his wife Amelia, also 60, and daughter Millie, 22.

At 2.15pm on Tuesday 9 February that year, PC McShane was cycling on his beat along Villiers Road when he met Millie Linden-Hitchcock, who told him she was concerned about her parents. She explained that she had left home for work at eight o'clock that morning, leaving her parents in the kitchen with everything quite normal.

She returned home for lunch at five minutes past one but found the front door locked. The key was always left under a piece of wood when they went out, but it was not there and she received no reply to her repeated knocking, lasting nearly half an hour. A box of eggs and two bottles of milk, delivered that morning, had not been taken inside and that was unusual as her mother was particular about such things. Millie had, of course, been expected home by her parents.

She then went to her sister's house in Romsey Road, where she told her the position and had her lunch. They assumed that their parents had gone out taking the key with them and it was on her way back to work that she met PC McShane. She told him she was now concerned and asked if he would check the house for her.

He went direct to 235 Millbrook Road and getting no answer to his knocking, obtained permission from a neighbour to climb over their rear fence into the garden of the Linden-Hitchcocks' house. He entered by the back door, which was unlocked, and found both the Linden-Hitchcocks in the kitchen, clearly dead.

Mrs Linden-Hitchcock was lying on the floor, with her back to the fireplace and with an apron and dust cloth tied around her head. Her upper body was covered in blood, the consequence of a wide gaping gash in her throat. Mr Linden-Hitchcock, his throat also severed, was sprawled in an armchair with his legs straddled across his wife's body. On the floor nearby were a bloodstained razor and heavy flat iron. An investigation, carried out by Inspector Carr, Shirley Division, established that there was no reason to believe anybody else was involved.

An inquest was held at the Civic Centre by the Borough Coroner, Mr Arthur Emanuel, on 18 February 1937, when evidence given by several witnesses gave some background to the tragedy. The inquest had been adjourned because the daughter was under medical treatment as a result of the tragedy.

Millie then explained that her parents had separated the previous April but had got back together in November. Although they always showed the greatest consideration for each other, her father had appeared very upset at times. He often said strange things, such as believing that somebody was coming to take him away. He had never got over his experiences in the Great War.

Dr Jack Hughes said he had attended Mr Linden-Hitchcock the previous November, finding him to be in a state of severe depression. He made a number of subsequent visits, each time discovering him in the same state, and had, in fact, considered certifying him as insane, but thought he had not quite reached that stage.

Dr Alex Russell, pathologist, when questioned, confirmed that Mrs Linden-Hitchcock's head injuries were so severe, with her skull fractured, that she must have

been rendered unconscious at once, before her throat was cut, and that Mr Linden-Hitchcock would not have lived long after his throat was severed.

The doctor thought that the woman would have died first. The jury, not unnaturally, returned a verdict that Thomas Linden-Hitchcock murdered his wife and then committed suicide, being of unsound mind.

The couple are both buried in Southampton Old Cemetery in grave P138-158.

The inscription on the headstone reads:

235 Millbrook Road. (*Southern Daily Echo*)

IN MEMORY OF MUM & DAD

THOMAS JAMES & AMELIA LINDEN-HITCHCOCK

DIED 9TH FEBRUARY 1937 AGED 60 YEARS

AND OF

THOMAS GILBERT & GEORGE JAMES LINDEN-HITCHCOCK

THE LOSS WAS SUDDEN, THE SHOCK SEVERE

TO LOSE THEM BOTH, WE LOVE SO DEAR

OUR LOSS SO GREAT, WE WILL NOT COMPLAIN

BUT TRUST IN GOD, TO MEET AGAIN

1943 – GEORGE ISAAC ABRAHAMS – TOO YOUNG TO HANG

By 1943 Southampton had sustained more than its fair share of attacks by German bombers in the wartime 'blitzkreig'. With over 5,000 high explosive bombs and 61,000 incendiaries dropped on the town since the start of the war, Southampton was a dangerous place to live in. Residents nevertheless played their part in the war effort. One such was former railway worker, George Isaac Abrahams, who, although aged 79, was one of the many brave volunteers who carried out fire-watching duties.

George's duties were carried out in the offices of the General Accident, Fire and Life Assurance Company at 14 Cumberland Place. It involved patrolling the premises during the night as several hundred incendiaries were likely to be dropped on the town during an air raid, and if any fell on the building they could be quickly extinguished. He was equipped with buckets of sand, a long handled scoop to remove a small incendiary and take it outside, as well as a stirrup pump that could be inserted into a bucket of water to extinguish a small fire.

George left his home in York Street, Northam, on Tuesday 23 February and arrived for duty at 6pm. He there met the office caretaker, Herbert Spain, who lived in a flat next door to the offices. The two men were in good spirits and spent some time singing

Cumberland Place *c.*1910. (*Eric Gadd*).

wartime songs together. At 7.30pm Herbert left George and went to his flat for his evening meal. As was his normal custom, he left the rear door of the office block unfastened, with George left alone in the building.

At about five minutes to eight he heard shouting outside and looking through his window across the garden saw George standing in the rear doorway. He was shouting, 'Help – Murder' and holding his head in his hands as he staggered about, bleeding heavily from the top of his head. Herbert went down and entered the rear door, following a trail of blood until he found George in the chief clerk's office, conscious but bleeding profusely from the top centre of his head. He was able to describe his attacker, who was young and with an amputated left hand, and said he had been hit on the head with the handle of a bayonet.

Herbert did his best to bandage George's head, called for an ambulance and when it arrived George was taken to the Royal South Hants Hospital. By the time he arrived he was unconscious and was immediately operated on, the surgeon finding that a piece of skull, the size of a sixpenny piece, had been driven right down into Mr Abrahams' brain.

Detective Sergeant Gordon Baker attended the scene, after George had been taken to hospital, and Herbert Spain showed him a bloodstained bayonet he had found on the floor of the chief clerk's office. It had not been there earlier.

Although the operation was partially successful George did not regain consciousness and died two days later, on Thursday 25 February. The cause of death was established as a depressed fracture of the skull, shock, cerebral haemorrhage and laceration of the brain tissue, all caused by a single blow.

Det.Sgt Baker interviewed all members of the office staff the morning after the attack and was told by a young employee that he had a conversation some

Gordon Baker in the early 1950s, as a uniformed superintendent. (*Janet Holloway*)

months earlier with a friend, in the course of which he had revealed the location of the keys of the office safe. This friend was Cyril Charles Lakeland, 17, who lived in Hazelbury Road, Totton. Lakeland had lost his left hand in a shunting accident on the railway in June the previous year and was therefore quickly arrested.

He initially denied all knowledge of the attack and said he was with his fiancée, Amy Lane, 18, at the time. He added they were at her sister's house in Elgin Road. However, when told that they would all be interviewed, he said, 'You win, I did it.' He then made a statement in which he said that four months earlier a friend who worked in the Cumberland Place offices had told him where the keys to the safe were kept. He therefore intended to rob the safe on an evening, when he knew that the premises would only be occupied by an elderly firewatcher.

He was deeply in debt, so on the evening of the attack he went to the office block with Amy, leaving her outside, saying he was going to see a friend. He had taken a small case with him, to put money in from the safe, also a bayonet owned by Amy's brother-in-law, Alfred Broughall, which he had taken from their house in Elgin Road. He said he took the bayonet in case the drawer containing the key was locked. He then entered by the unlocked rear door and hid under the stairs, seeing the fire-watcher pass by in the dark with his torch on.

The site of the redeveloped former office block at 14 Cumberland Place, next to what is now the Southampton Park Hotel (called the Royal Hotel in 1943), and the rear alley used by Lakeland to gain access to the unlocked rear door.

Lakeland said he then entered the office and was going towards the desk when the firewatcher returned. In his own words, 'When he came round something came over me and I hit him on the head with the bayonet.' He then ran out of the building, met Amy, told her what had happened and they both ran across the road, through the parks and home. She saw that he had blood on his hand and a heavily bloodstained handkerchief, which he later burnt.

Lakeland was then charged with the murder and appeared before Mr Justice Singleton at the Central Criminal Court (The Old Bailey) on Friday 2 April 1943. He pleaded 'not guilty' and the jury of 12, including four women, were first told that because Lakeland had not yet reached the age of 18 he did not run the risk of being hanged. Mr John Maude, prosecuting counsel, said 'this therefore took away a great deal of anxiety in the case'.

Amy Lane gave evidence, as did her sister Phoebe Broughall and her husband Alfred, who was an ARP despatch rider. He identified the bayonet as his property, brought home from the war as a souvenir, and Lakeland's youthful indiscretion was then revealed. Amazingly, prior to the attack, he had told them all of his intention of going to the office block to get money from the safe. They had advised him not to do it but he had replied, 'Don't worry, there's only one old man there'.

Lakeland's defending counsel, Mr Scott Henderson, did not call any evidence for the defence, submitting that the killing amounted to manslaughter, not murder, as Lakeland did not have the intention to kill. 'The blow struck was unpremeditated and the jury could not be satisfied that Lakeland had the intent to cause grievous bodily harm.'

The jury, however, found him guilty of murder, but with a recommendation of mercy on account of his age. He was then sentenced to be detained 'during His Majesty's pleasure'.

George Isaac Abrahams is buried in Southampton Old Cemetery in unmarked grave D184-246

1949 – JOAN ANDREWS – SHOT BY A WAR HERO

Joan Vivienne Veronica Callen spent her childhood living with her parents at 1, Honeysuckle Road, Bassett, a council house in Southampton's 'Flower Estate'. She was 18 at the outbreak of World War Two and soon after she met Peter J.S. Holt, a serviceman. After a whirlwind

courtship they married in Southampton towards the end of 1942, but Peter was discharged from the service and unexpectedly died towards the end of 1944.

Joan was left a widow, with a baby daughter, Jeanette, but a year later she met 25-year-old Donald Andrews, DFC, a fair-haired, but balding, RAF Flight Lieutenant. They fell in love and a year later, in late 1946, when she was aged 25, they married in Shropshire, where he was serving.

Joan Andrews. (*Southern Daily Echo*)

Their married life was, to all outward appearances, stable and happy, but there were facts about her husband of which she was unaware.

Donald Owen Andrews had a troubled childhood. In 1937, at the age of 17 and while studying for his Higher School Certificate in Southampton, he had a major nervous breakdown. He imagined that he had killed his mother and, remarkably, had also killed himself. It was so severe that he was sent to Park Prewett Mental Institution, where he remained for 10 months. However, on his discharge he recovered sufficiently to obtain work as an assistant in a store in Above Bar and on the outbreak of World War Two volunteered for the RAF.

He clearly did not present a problem during his medical examination as he was commissioned as a Flight Lieutenant, fought in Coastal Command with distinction during the Battle of Britain and was awarded the Distinguished Flying Cross for his bravery.

In 1944, while serving in West Africa, he contracted infantile paralysis but fully recovered.

Donald continued to serve in the RAF as a navigator, until discharged in July 1948, by which time the couple had a baby son, Michael John. The family then moved to Winchester Road, Southampton where they lived with Donald's father, Joseph, a fishmonger in Shirley. Joseph had been a War Reserve Constable in the Southampton County Borough police force.

Donald Andrews.
(*Southern Daily Echo*)

Donald did not obtain employment following his discharge from the RAF and by July 1949 had serious money worries. He received letters about debts from the Midland Bank, from a firm of bookmakers and from a solicitor writing on behalf of Tote Investors Ltd, demanding payment of £13. This seems to have seriously affected Andrews, who believed he was going to be prosecuted over the debts. Up to now he and his wife had enjoyed a happy relationship.

However, at 6.15am on the morning of 22 July Mr Andrews senior got up to make himself a cup of tea and heard two unusual popping noises upstairs.

The Andrews family home in Winchester Road.

He went up, knocked on the bedroom door where his son, daughter-in-law and their baby slept, and his son told him to come in. Donald was standing by the bed, partly dressed, and immediately said, 'You had better call the police dad, I have shot Joan'. Joseph then saw that Mrs Andrews was lying on the bed, with a severely injured head on a bloodstained pillow. He took Donald downstairs, made him a cup of tea to calm him down and phoned Shirley police station.

Shirley police station. (*Hampshire Constabulary History Society*)

PC Bob Rackley arrived shortly after, spoke to Joseph Andrews and then saw that Mrs Andrews appeared dead. He found a .38 service revolver under her bed. It contained three live and two spent cartridges and smelt of burnt cordite, as though recently fired. He took the gun downstairs and said to Donald Andrews, 'Is this the gun you used?' and he replied, 'Yes, that's it'. He was then cautioned. P/Sgt Bill Fisk arrived, checked on the situation and told Donald he was under arrest. He replied, 'This is the worst part of it; get me away as quickly as possible'. He was then taken to Shirley police station.

On arrival he was seen by Det.Sgt George Adams and Det.Insp Bert Gibbons, who cautioned him and asked for an explanation. Donald then said, 'You will see that I was going to be prosecuted for debt. I have drawn out all the money we had in our joint account, without her knowledge, and I could not bear her to know. I knew it would upset her. I was the only one who drew on the account and there is nothing left. It was 10 days ago I decided to do it, three times I made preparation but at the last moment I could not do it. Then I woke up at 5 o'clock this morning, lay there thinking about it; then I got up and shot her.

I had three alternatives, the first was to do what I did; the second, I could leave her, but that would have been too cruel and I could not hurt her that way – she was very fond of me; and the third was to come to the police and ask for protective custody, to save me doing the sort of thing I have done.'

Mrs Andrews was then seen by the police surgeon, Dr Grimston, who confirmed her death and that she had been shot twice in the right temple, the second bullet entering the same hole as the first. Two spent bullets were later found in the pillow by Det.Sgt George Adams.

He was then charged by Det.Sgt Adams with the murder of Joan Andrews and after several remand appearances was committed on 12 August for trial at the Hampshire Assizes, where he appeared before Mr Justice Byrne on 19 December 1949 and pleaded not guilty.

He was defended by J. Casswell, KC, who called Dr John Blorach, a specialist psychiatrist at Park Prewett Mental Hospital, where Andrews had been a patient.

The doctor stated that Andrews was suffering from schizophrenia, living in two different worlds, and at the time of the shooting did not know that what he was doing was wrong. He had suffered a relapse due to his financial worries.

The accused was not called to give evidence on his own behalf and Mr Casswell, defending, stated that Andrews, 'apparently unprovoked, without irritation or any adequate reason', had destroyed the person of someone he loved the most.

The jury, which included two women, retired for only 28 minutes before returning with a verdict of 'Guilty of murder but insane'. Mr Justice Byrne then ordered Andrews to be kept in custody, as a Broadmoor patient, 'until His Majesty's pleasure is known'.

Joan Andrews is buried in unmarked plot L7-182 in South Stoneham Cemetery.

1949 – ANNIE KNIGHT – LADY IN RED

Thomas Gibson, 55, a foreman ganger in the docks, took his wife for a walk in the early hours of Saturday 24 September 1949 because she was suffering from toothache and unable to sleep. At about 1.10am, on their way to their home at 2a Floating Bridge Road, they crossed Hoglands Park on a footpath alongside the cricket pitch. It was very dark and Thomas, a former amateur boxer and regimental sergeant major in the Black Watch, told his wife he did not like that spot at night so they should be careful.

They then saw a large black object on the grass, in the centre of the cricket pitch, with three men running away from it. As they got closer they saw the object appeared to be a woman huddled on the ground, so Thomas initially ran after the men, towards Hanover Buildings, but they were too fast for him. He returned to the woman, who was dressed in a red overcoat, and realised she was dead.

He therefore dialled '999' from a nearby telephone kiosk and when Inspector Ernie Carter arrived by police car took him to the scene. The inspector, who was due to retire the following day, saw that the woman was clearly dead, with severe facial injuries, and realising that the death was not natural, radioed for assistance.

He was soon joined by Det.Ch.Insp. Gordon Baker and the Chief Constable, Charles Box.

They decided the body would be better examined in daylight by a pathologist, so it was covered by a tent made from tarpaulin, with the area cordoned off, and

Chief Constable Charles Box, OBE.

uniformed officers posted to prevent the public crossing the path around the pitch. Dr H.H. Gleave, pathologist, examined the body later that morning and it was taken to the Royal South Hants Hospital for a more detailed examination.

Dr Gleave found the woman had died from shock, haemorrhage from a fractured jaw and inhalation of blood. Her cheeks were bruised, her lips were swollen and slightly cut, she had two black eyes, a large bruise on the right temple, a small bruise to the forehead and extensive bruising on both sides of the neck, under the jaw. The marks on the neck suggested a tight gripping of the throat, with the fracture of a bone in the windpipe suggesting considerable pressure. He thought she had sustained at least four blows, with at least one of them so severe that pieces of the broken jaw were actually driven inside her mouth.

Det.Con. Basil Ballard also attended the scene of the attack and found, under the

second bench from the cricket pavilion, seven shillings and nine pence neatly piled, together with an ordinary table knife and a bloodstained headscarf.

Further away, near a cricket sight screen, he found a black handbag and a green and red shopping bag. He also took samples of blood he found on the bench, on the ground near the bench and the ground in the centre of the cricket pitch.

Det.Con. Basil Ballard.
(*Hampshire Constabulary History Society*)

Enquiries were made in the vicinity, starting with the Hoglands Park Nissen huts that were next to the footpath adjoining the cricket pitch. They were erected as

The second bench from the cricket pavilion, the scene of the attack.

The Hoglands Park cricket pitch. The trees in the background cover an area that still contained wartime Nissen huts in 1949.

headquarters for the wartime American 14th Major Port Embarkation Unit. At the end of World War Two they were used as temporary accommodation for local residents who had lost their homes in the bombing.

A wartime photograph, taken by the US Provost Marshal, the late Captain Dalton Newfield, showing the entrance of the path adjoining the cricket pitch, with some of the Nissen huts in the background, and the same view in 2011.

One of the residents, Mrs Gertrude Whale, whose address was given as Hut No.9, The Hutments, Hoglands Park, was seen and she said at about 11.35pm on the Friday she had seen and heard an argument from her window between a man and a woman sitting on a bench about five yards away, facing the cricket park. The woman appeared most abusive and swearing a lot.

She heard the man say, 'You've got my money' while holding her by the throat and hitting her in the face. The woman then fell off the bench but the man continued to hit her four or five times while she was on the ground. Two men then walked along the path, so he stopped hitting her and crouched over her, in almost a lying position.

After the men had passed he hit her again several times, stopped and looked at her, then picked her up bodily and carried her in his arms about 50 yards, to the middle of the cricket pitch, where he put her on the ground. He then returned to the bench, picked up his raincoat and walked away, towards the pavilion.

As a result of this interview the investigating officers dropped their enquiries into the three men seen running away from the scene by Thomas Gibson. They were satisfied the men had probably seen the body but were frightened of becoming involved.

The woman in red was well-known to the police. She was 5ft 3in Annie Knight, 48, of Brunswick Square, a well known local prostitute, and this was confirmed by documents in the handbag found at the scene. She had raven-black curly hair and was slightly crippled, with a clumped heel. Generally known as 'Hoppy', the police knew her to be a quarrelsome woman who usually carried a table knife in her handbag.

Annie had been separated from her husband, Sidney John Knight, a night watchman, for the past two years and he identified her body at the public mortuary.

Annie Knight. (*Southern Daily Echo*)

The murder investigation took a dramatic turn at 10.45am that day when Edward Long, 26, a labourer living in the Salvation Army Hostel, Bond Street, walked into the Docks police station. He saw P/Sgt Colin Lester and said, 'I went out with a woman with a red coat who walked with a limp last night and I heard this morning that she had been murdered.'

He went on to say, after the sergeant had cautioned him, that he had met her in the street and gone into the park with her. The inference was that this was for the purpose of prostitution. However, he then found that 7s 9d had been taken from his pocket and the woman refused to return it. Edward said she then screamed and pulled out a knife, so he hit her.

Det.Ch.Insp. Gordon Baker then saw Long at the Docks police station and took him to police headquarters at the Civic Centre. On the way Long said, several times, 'Would you think that you could kill a woman with your fist?' After arrival he made a written statement, in which he said 'I heard that a woman had been killed in the parks, what I told the sergeant was true, I didn't know it was the same woman. I just had to go and give myself up. I picked her up near the parks and went to a seat with her. I had seven or eight shillings in my pocket. I walked away and left her, and found my money had gone, I knew she had it. I went back and said "Give me my money"; she screamed and took the knife out of her bag. I hit her and knocked her off the seat, picked her up and hit her again.

I went through her handbag and could not find the money. I picked her up and carried her out into the middle of the park. We were near a path. I went back to the seat and picked up her two bags. I went through one but could not get my money, so I threw them down near the cricket screen and walked halfway to the Salvation Army and then went back to the park again and found she had gone. I thought she had picked herself up and gone off. I had drunk 16 or 17 pints of a mix of beer and cider, but was not drunk. Do you think that two blows would kill her?'

He was then seen by the police surgeon, who saw that Long's right hand was badly swollen, extending up towards the wrist. He also had blood on his clothing, which was taken to the Metropolitan Police Laboratory for forensic examination. It was later found that Long's trousers and jacket were heavily bloodstained with blood of Annie Knight's blood group, which was different to that of Edward Long's. Bloodstains in the park and on the bench were also the same group as Annie Knight's.

He was then charged with the murder and appeared before Mr Justice Byrne at the Hampshire Assizes on Friday 9 December 1949, when he pleaded 'not guilty'.

Following a two-day trial the jury retired for 23 minutes before returning with a verdict of 'not guilty of murder but guilty of manslaughter'. Mr Justice Byrne told Long that the jury had taken a merciful view of the case but it was a violent brutal assault he had made on the woman. He then sentenced him to seven years imprisonment.

Annie Knight is buried in Hollybrook Cemetery, in unmarked grave B9-185.

1952 – MARY ANDERSON – A DISSENTING JURY FOREMAN

Mr Douglas Harfield was a very experienced coroner (well known to the author) with an air of absolute authority, but he was taken aback when boldly challenged by clerk David Loring, the foreman of an adjourned inquest held on Friday 18 July 1952.

The circumstances were that Mary Anderson, 25, a native of Newcastle who suffered

from tuberculosis, and Andrew Dick, 28, had been found dead in a coal gas-filled furnished room in Denzil Avenue on Wednesday 9 July 1952.

They were discovered at 9am that day by 13-year-old George Llewellyn, the landlady's son, who had gone to call them because they had failed to arrive for breakfast. The couple had lived there, as Mr and Mrs Dick, for three years. Andrew, a married man and a native of Glasgow, was a deckhand with the Red Funnel Line steamer *Medina*.

The Denzil Avenue house.

The police were called and took possession of two handwritten notes found in the room, later confirmed written by Andrew.

One note was addressed to Mary Anderson's mother and said: 'Mrs Scott, I am sorry this is the only way out. I have had Mary in hospital but she would only stay there two weeks. It would have taken six months or more to cure her. She was no sooner out of hospital until she was in the "Groom" again, that was where I found her last night. There was an awful quarrel and it has come out like this. But I will give her God's blessing, because she will need it, and so will I. I will not sign myself as 'Andy' because it would not be right.'

(The 'Groom' mentioned in the letter was the Horse & Groom public house in East Street.)

The second letter was addressed to the coroner and read: 'I am not very good at spelling but you will have to take it as you find it. Just now I am not dead, but by the time you read this letter I intend to be. Right away you put it down 'suicide' and Mary Anderson was strangled. You will be perfectly right and make sure you put it down. I was unbalanced because I am sure no one could do such a thing if they were in sane mind. I am indeed sorry that I have put you to all this trouble but life can't go on like this. Your obedient servant, Mr A. Dick.'

Dr Grimston, the police surgeon, who had attended the scene, stated the couple had both died in the early hours of the morning. He told the jury that Mary was lying in bed, with her arms folded across her chest, fully clothed except for her shoes, and a subsequent post-mortem revealed small lacerations on her chin and forehead, and a deeper laceration on the back of her head. There were purple marks on the neck, indicating bleeding under the skin and consistent with manual strangulation.

Andrew Dick was on a blanket spread on the bedroom floor, his head on a pillow and his wrists slashed. There was blood on his arms, shoulders and chest. Coal gas was escaping

Eric Coleman, who retired as Chief Superintendent.

from a small tube that had been disconnected from a gas ring and was close to Andrew's head.

The doctor told the jury, 'In my view the man murdered the woman by manual strangulation and subsequently committed suicide by cutting both radial arteries and suffocating himself with the fumes of coal gas.'

He also said that Mary Anderson had been suffering from tuberculosis and if she had been healthy the pressure on her throat might not have killed her.

P/Sgt Eric Coleman said he found strips of paper folded to fit under the door and paper placed across the fireplace.

The coroner asked the landlady, Mrs Llewellyn, if the couple quarrelled and was told that they did quarrel, on two occasions she had to call the police.

She added, 'He was rather a quick tempered man. He threatened before to take her life. He had beaten her wickedly on previous occasions. Sometimes the quarrels were about money.'

At the end of the evidence the jury retired for half an hour and on their return the foreman, David Loring, said their verdict was that the woman died through manual strangulation, accelerated by her condition, and that the strangulation was done by the man. He added that Dick committed suicide while of unsound mind.

HM Coroner then said he proposed to record the verdicts as murder and suicide, but the foreman remarked 'But we didn't say the word "murder"', to which the coroner replied 'But you must do so Mr Foreman'. Mr Loring then pointed out that the medical evidence was that the pressure used would not have caused death if she had been healthy and Dick might not have had the deliberate intent to kill her.

HM Coroner said he was empowered to accept a majority verdict and that if Mr Loring wished dissent from it he need not sign the form on which the verdict was presented. 'It is a free country'. The remaining eight members of the jury, without Mr Loring, then signed the form declaring the verdict to be murder and suicide.

1956 – ANGELA RENNIE – 'A TRAGEDY AS OPPOSED TO A FELONY'

Charles Alec Rennie, 41, a dry cleaner's agent of Leaside Way, Bassett, sustained a serious head injury in October 1944, during World War Two, when a piece of shrapnel penetrated the left side of his head. A piece of his brain the size of a florin was found protruding from his skull and this was removed during an operation. He had a further operation to remove some remaining bone chips and a repair of the skull by covering the hole with a metal plate in January 1945.

As a result of this terrible injury, he suffered from severe headaches and bouts of dizziness, but this did not prevent him marrying Audrey Wade in Middlesex in 1944, following his discharge from the army. Their daughter, Angela Marion, was born in 1946 in Hitchin, Hertfordshire, and the family subsequently moved to Southampton in 1952, where they obtained a 'pre-fab' at 117, Leaside Way, Bassett Green. The prefabricated homes were a single-storey World War Two idea, made of wood, metal and plaster, with no house bricks.

Charles Rennies' troubles increased in 1955 when his wife Audrey developed severe psychological problems, resulting in her being admitted to Ravenswood Mental Hospital, Fareham, on Wednesday 25 January 1956. Her condition was no doubt brought about by the fact that Charles had periodic fits of extreme temper, in the course of which he would sometimes attack his wife. He was also known to have punched the plaster wall of their 'pre-fab', on one occasion putting his fist almost through the wall.

Former typical 'pre-fabs' in Southampton. (*Bitterne Local History Society*)

Modern housing in Leaside Way, on the site of the former 'pre-fab' No. 117.

His father-in-law, Bertram Wade, also heard Charles say, several times, that he had 200 aspirins already crushed up and was going to take 100 himself and the give other 100 to Angela so she would die with him. But Mr Wade did not take the threats seriously.

His next door neighbour, Mrs Alberta Hampton, spoke to Charles on Sunday 29 January and saw he appeared to be extremely concerned. He told her that his wife was very ill, and his mother was dying with cancer and said, 'I just don't know which way to turn'.

On the morning of the following day, Monday 30 January, Rita Gibson, who regularly acted as a general help for the family, made her usual visit and Charles left for work at 1pm. He mentioned that he had seen his wife at Ravenswood Hospital the previous day and she did not appear at all well. Mrs Gibson then took nine-year-old Angela to school, leaving the house for home at 1.20pm.

When she called again at 9am the following morning she saw the blinds were still drawn and had no answer to her knocking. She then made enquiries at Angela's school and found that she had not arrived that morning, so became very concerned and decided to call the police. A constable attended, forced an entry via a front window and discovered Charles' dead body, in his pyjamas, next to that of a clearly dead Angela, in the front bedroom, lying side by side in bed. CID were immediately informed and Det.Sgt Bill Dodd attended at 1pm. He saw that Charles had serious injuries to his throat and on a table alongside the bed were two glasses containing heavy brown sediment. A two-edged safety razor blade was on the bed, with blood spots leading from the girl, round the bed to the side where Charles was lying. There were also four empty aspirin bottles and an empty beer bottle on the kitchen draining board.

Det.Sgt Dodd searched some clothing he found in the adjacent living room and found two notes in a wallet. Undated and addressed to his neighbour, Mrs Richards, they showed that Charles initially intended to take his own life away from home at the time of writing and did not intend his daughter to also die. He asked Mrs Richards to look after his daughter and, if necessary, adopt her, so for some unknown reason Charles clearly changed his mind.

Evidence was given that Dr Richard Goodbody, pathologist, had examined the bodies at the public mortuary and found Charles had cuts on his wrists and fingertips, and a very deep cut in his throat. The post-mortem also revealed that he had taken a quantity of powdered aspirin, but death was due to haemorrhage from a severed artery in his throat. Young Angela had a one inch cut in her throat, insufficient to severe an artery, but three small marks on the front of her neck suggested they were made by fingernails. She had bruised neck muscles and death was due to asphyxia. It was clear she had been strangled.

At the subsequent inquest, held on 24 February 1956, HM Coroner, Mr D.B. Harefield, said, 'I think you will agree that this is definitely a tragedy as opposed to a felony. Frankly, that is how I look at it.' The jury later returned verdicts of murder of Angela by her father, who had then committed suicide while the balance of his mind was disturbed.

Both Charles and Angela Rennie are buried in South Stoneham Cemetery, in unmarked grave P4-95.

1973 – ALEXANDER SNEDDON SMITH – A WIFE'S 26 YEARS OF MISERY

By December 1973, Alexander Smith, 54, had subjected his wife, Elsa Nancy, 48, a former nurse, to 26 years of torment. He had not held a job for more than a year over the previous 23 years and she had been the target of repeated acts of violence. A heavy drinker, almost an alcoholic, he was prone to outbursts of violent rage when drunk. At Christmas 1959, Elsa had to be taken to hospital to have her face stitched after he had struck her. At the New Year, 1970, while she was recovering from an operation, he beat and kicked her. On another occasion he smacked her violently in the face because he complained she was slow in getting him a cup of tea. There is no doubt that Elsa had suffered considerably, but she still stuck by her promise 'to love and obey'.

During the evening of 7 December 1973, after Alexander drank some whisky at home, the couple went out with their daughter, Mrs Susan Gordon, and her husband.

Alexander won £60 at a bingo club, and after a celebratory meal at George's Restaurant in town, they returned to the family home in Cherwell Crescent, Millbrook.

The Smith family home.

Mr and Mrs Gordon then heard loud shouting from an adjoining room, and when they ran in to see what was up they found Alexander Smith moaning and bleeding heavily from his chest. Mr Gordon saw that Elsa was holding a knife in her hand, so he took it from her and threw it into the garden.

Alexander insisted on being taken to a nearby neighbour's house, from where an ambulance was called. He was taken to the General Hospital, where it was discovered he had a stab wound, several inches deep, in his left chest, entering the left ventricle of his heart. He was operated on immediately and made a fair recovery.

The police had attended and when they questioned Elsa Smith she said, 'I meant to kill him. He had a tie in his hand, saying he was going to strangle me. I got a knife from my bag and stabbed him. I should have killed him. I have been a nurse and knew where to do it. I have had 26 years of him. He has beaten me and the children. He gets drunk and violent; I could not take any more.'

She was then charged with attempted murder and appeared at the Magistrates Court the following day, when she was bailed. However, Alexander's condition deteriorated and despite medical attention he died on Christmas Eve.

Elsa was thus further charged with murder and, after a committal in custody, appeared before Mr Justice Wien at the Winchester Crown Court on 1 April 1974. Alexander had, by then, been cremated. Her plea of 'not guilty' to the murder of her husband but 'guilty' to manslaughter on the grounds of provocation was accepted by Mr Edward Laughton Scott, QC, for the prosecution.

The judge then told her, 'You have led, I have no doubt, a miserable life for something like 26 years. But domestic dispute, however long endured, can never amount to a licence to kill a partner. I have no doubt you suffered a complete, though temporary, loss of control. Taking everything into consideration, I think normal compassion and humanity require that you should not be deprived of your liberty.'

He then placed her on probation for two years.

1976 – IVY MAY BAILEY – EXTREME INSANE JEALOUSY

At an inquest, held at the Coroner's Court, Civic Centre, on 19 August 1976, a tale of very extreme jealousy unfolded before the jury when extracts were read from the diary of 65-year-old divorcee Albert Edward Nicholson. Albert was a married man with two adopted children but had left his wife in 1966. He was known to be a violent man towards his family and both the son and daughter had left home because of his behaviour.

The jury were told that the diary was divided into three sections called 'How I met her', 'How we fell in love' and 'I come to live at her home'. It had been found at Nicholson's flat in Lawn Road, Portswood, together with several letters. They all related to 58-year-old Mrs Ivy May Bailey, a canteen assistant, living in Kendal Avenue, Millbrook. Ivy was also a married woman, married to her second husband, Harry Bailey, but had separated from him nine years ago. She had two children from her first marriage and two from the second.

The two had met in 1966 when both were working at IBM in Millbrook. They formed a strong relationship and Albert moved into her home in Kendal Avenue. However, his possessiveness proved too much for Ivy and he left the house in 1972, moving into lodgings in Lawn Road.

On Friday 23 July 1976 they met at the Freemantle Working Men's Club and left to go to Ivy's house in Kendal Avenue. Relatives in the house saw Albert's car parked outside the house, but it was then seen driven away with Ivy in the passenger's seat. She failed to return home that night and the following morning her son-in-law reported her missing. Routine police enquiries were made, without result, and the following Saturday afternoon Ivy's relatives went to Albert's flat in Lawn Road and forced an entry.

It was then that they found the diaries and letters, the contents of which disturbed them as they appeared to indicate Albert intended to murder Ivy and then commit suicide. Det.Sgt Desmond Breese arranged for a full-scale search to be carried out, as a result of which Albert's red Cortina car was found at 3.15pm by PC Michael Whitcher parked in a service road alongside Millbrook Recreation Ground.

The car was locked on the inside and the keys were in the ignition. Albert could be seen slumped forward in the driving seat with a covering over his head. A single barrel sawn-off 410 shotgun was between his feet with the barrel resting against his right shoulder. It was obvious that he was dead and that the gun had been placed in his mouth before being fired.

Ivy's dead body was in the passenger seat with her hands folded in her lap and a handkerchief covering her face. When the car was forced open it was found that she had been shot in the head near her right ear.

The service road alongside Millbrook Recreation Ground.

A letter had been left on the car dashboard, in which Albert Nicholson said he could not live without Mrs Bailey, whose nickname was 'Mick'. It was read to the jury by HM Coroner Mr Harry Roe, and it said 'To the police. I parked here last night Fri at 11.30. After I shot my 'Mick' when we left the Freemantle Club, the reason why did not do myself was that I wanted to keep her with me as long as I could. Why I did this can be answered in letter I left at my flat, the keys are with this note. I cannot go on living without her. I only see her a few times a week at the club. We are never on our own, like we were three years ago. I loved and adored her. Bert Nicholson'.

John Bailey, of Kent Street, Northam, Mrs Bailey's youngest son, gave evidence that his mother had asked Nicholson to leave her home because he had created angry scenes and did not get on with the others in the family. John Bailey stated that Nicholson was 'a terribly jealous man' and became upset if others did anything for Mrs Bailey.

On the night she was killed she had intended going away the following day to Devon, on holiday with others in the family, but Nicholson wanted her to go alone with him. It seems that in his demented mind the only solution was to kill her and himself. The jury, not unnaturally, returned a verdict that Albert Nicholson murdered Ivy Bailey and then killed himself. Albert was later cremated.

Ivy Bailey is buried in Hollybrook Cemetery, in plot K13-208, and the headstone reads:

TREASURED MEMORIES

OF

OUR DEAR MUM

IVY MAY BAILEY

(MICK)

FELL ASLEEP 23RD JULY 1976

AGED 58 YEARS

1976 – LARAINE KATHLEEN DODDS – A SAVAGE OBSESSION

It started at 1pm on 20 August 1976 with a dramatic '999' call saying a man was threatening to leap to his death from a balcony on the 12th floor of the Millbank House tower block in Northam. He was Christopher Malcom Tancred, 24, of Ailsa Lane, Itchen and the drama continued for more than six hours.

Ignoring the pleas of police officers he continued to sway over the balcony, high over the shopping precinct, until 7.20pm, when he was pulled to safety by Mr Reg Hampton. Mr Hampton had climbed from an adjoining balcony and coaxed him into the arms of waiting police officers.

Tancred had gained access to the building by knocking on the door of the upper flat on the pretext of asking for a glass of water. He had then gone through the flat and climbed onto the balcony wall.

The 15-storey Millbank House, with the exterior re-clad by the City Council and the former balconies now completely enclosed.

The reason for Tancred's threatened suicide was revealed when he was questioned by the police. He admitted having killed his girlfriend, Laraine Kathleen Dodds, 21, a shop manageress, at his home in Ailsa Lane and had intended to kill himself. She was separated from her husband and had recently moved to temporary accommodation in Tranby Road, Itchen.

However, she had left her flat a few days earlier and moved into the house in Ailsa Lane to stay with Tancred and his father. He had known her for about six months and was convinced that she had become pregnant, either by him or some other man. She had denied being pregnant, stating that she had been tested negative, but he refused to accept this and they had quarrelled as a result. It was quickly apparent that this was a severe obsession with him.

Police went to the address in Ailsa Lane and found the girl's badly injured body, lying on her back, in a ground floor bedroom of the semi-detached house. Tancred had admitted stabbing and cutting her with two knives, as well as hitting her on the head with a hammer.

The two knives, one with a broken blade, and a hammer, were on the floor near the body. A subsequent post-mortem by Dr Richard Goodbody revealed stab wounds to the stomach and chest, slashing wounds to the neck and signs of hammer blows to the head.

Det.Supt Cyril 'Tank' Holdaway, head of Hampshire CID, led the investigation and Tancred was later charged with the murder. He appeared before Mr Justice Cobb at the Hampshire Assizes, Winchester, on 20 December 1976, and pleaded 'not guilty' to murder but 'guilty' to manslaughter by reason of diminished responsibility.

The Tancred family home.

Christopher Malcolm Tancred.
(*Hampshire Constabulary
History Society*)

Det. Supt Cyril
Holdaway.

The court was told that the deceased girl had not, in fact, been pregnant and that their relationship had been strained because of his jealousy and obsessive and pathological fear that she was pregnant by him or someone else.

The judge, after reading reports from three psychiatrists, told Tancred that he had committed 'a brutal and savage killing of that young girl' but was suffering from an abnormality of the mind. He then ordered him to be detained at Broadmoor Prison under Section 60 of the Mental Health Act.

Laraine Dodds is buried in St Mary's Extra Cemetery, Portsmouth Road, in plot H18-177 and the headstone reads:

CHERISHED MEMORIES

– OF –

LARAINE KATHLEEN

DODDS (NÉE HOOK)

DEAREST DAUGHTER OF

BETTY AND LEN,

SISTER OF TERESA

CRUELLY TAKEN

AUGUST 20TH 1976

AGED 21 YEARS

GOD BLESS DARLING

R.I.P.

ALSO

BETTY JOYCE

HOOK (NÉE FROST)

DIED 7-1-82

AGED 51 YEARS

GOODNIGHT GOD BLESS

1983 – CATHERINE MAY BELL – A BRUTAL AND SAVAGE ATTACK

Catherine May Bell, 49, suffered from multiple sclerosis and lived with her husband, Alec Alan Bell, 48, in Grosvenor Close, Portswood. Sadly, her condition worsened over the years and by late 1982 she had the added burden of discovering that her husband, a Red Funnel booking clerk, had formed a relationship with one of the office cleaners.

As a result she commenced divorce proceedings and because of his violent behaviour the Southampton County Court made an Order restraining him from molesting her. On 5 April 1983 the same court also made an order requiring him to leave the house in Grosvenor Close within 14 days.

Later that same day, as a result of a '999' call, police were called and Det.Insp. Brian Paddison later went to the property where he saw Mrs Bell's body. She had sustained severe multiple injuries to her head, stomach and arms. He made immediate enquiries and as a result saw her husband, who admitted having killed his wife.

When questioned he revealed that he had struck her with both

The house in Grosvenor Close.

fists and feet, knocking her to the ground and had then stood directly on her chest. He was charged with her murder and appeared before Mr Justice Stocker at Winchester Crown Court on 8 December 1983, where he pleaded not guilty. The unfortunate Catherine Bell had by then been cremated.

Mr Charles Whitby, prosecuting, outlined the attack on Bell's crippled wife, and the jury, after a short trial, accepted the prosecution evidence and found him guilty of murder.

The judge stated, 'It was a brutal and savage attack on a defenceless woman' and sentenced him to life imprisonment.

1983 – JOHN GLENN – STABBED WITH A SABRE

John Glenn, 22, unemployed, who lived in Shakespeare Avenue, and unemployed slaughterman Thomas Francis Michael Brady Turnbull, 25, of Furzedown Road, were both Glaswegians who more than enjoyed a drink. On the evening of Thursday 24 March, 1983 the two of them spent the day and evening drinking heavily in various public houses, before returning late that night to Turnbull's flat in Furzedown Road. Turnbull had separated from his wife two days earlier and was in a despondent mood, having been left to care for his five-year-old daughter on his own.

Thomas Turnbull's home in Furzedown Road, Highfield.

Turnbull left the flat in the early hours to try to borrow cigarettes from a neighbour, and on his return found John Glenn eating food he had taken from the refrigerator without first asking permission. This greatly upset Turnbull, as he had bought it especially for his daughter, and the two got into a heated argument.

It resulted in Glenn punching Turnbull in the face, causing a violent reaction, with an antique sword hanging on the wall being snatched by Turnbull, who used it to stab Glenn in the body. It turned into a frenzied attack with the unfortunate Glenn ending up with a total of seven stab wounds, in the chest, abdomen, left armpit, left arm and left thigh. The stab wound in the chest penetrated between the first and second ribs, resulting in a severe cut in the pulmonary artery. This led to a massive loss of blood, with Glenn collapsing at the foot of the stairs in the main hallway.

A babysitter, obtained by Turnbull to look after his daughter while he was out drinking, witnessed the fight between the two men and saw Glenn stabbed and stumble down the stairs, sitting at the bottom with blood pouring from his side. Another flat resident came out, hearing the noise, and saw Glenn's unconscious body on the hallway floor.

The police were called, arriving soon after, at 2.25am, saw that Glenn was then dead and made immediate enquiries that resulted in Turnbull being arrested on suspicion of murder. He was taken to police headquarters where he said, after caution, 'It was all his fault. I bought him a drink tonight and he asked if he could stay at my place. The next thing I know he is stealing my daughter's food. I caught him doing it. I tried to throw him out but he started to fight. I have got a big sword as an ornament. I was so mad I picked it up and used it.'

Det.Insp. Bill Lawton was in charge of the investigation and Turnbull was charged with the murder. He appeared before Mr Justice Mann at Winchester Crown Court on Wednesday 5

October 1983, when he pleaded not guilty to murder but admitted manslaughter. His admission was not accepted by the prosecution and the case proceeded on the murder charge.

Dr David Adey, police surgeon, gave evidence of examining Turnbull at 5.10am on the day of the murder and stated the accused had told him he had drunk 15 pints of beer between 6.30pm the previous evening and 1.30am that morning, as well as sharing half a bottle of port. Turnbull also said he had been punched by Glenn after he caught him stealing food from his fridge and that he had killed him with a sword. The doctor told the court that Turnbull had a poor recollection of the events.

Turnbull gave evidence, saying he had drunk 15 pints of lager that night and told the story of catching Glenn stealing food from the fridge. He said, 'He started to struggle and I fell against the budgie's cage and knocked it over. I clipped the table and fell back. I picked up the sword; it had been hanging on the wall as an ornament. The next thing I remember is Glenn holding my hand I was holding the sword in and I threw it away. Glenn was just lying there, I could not believe it.'

At the conclusion of the evidence the jury found Turnbull guilty of the murder, and the court heard he had been sentenced to five years in a young offenders' institution by the Glasgow High Court in 1977 for offences of housebreaking and rape.

Mr Justice Mann, in sentencing Turnbull to life imprisonment, told him, 'The jury have found you guilty on what is in my view the plainest possible evidence of a sustained and brutal assault upon a man who was smaller than you.'

A sabre of the type used to stab John Glenn.

1985 – ANN HARNDEN – KILLED WITH A SAWN-OFF SHOTGUN

Mitchell Harnden, 36, was so infatuated with his wife Ann, 35, that when their marriage ran into serious difficulties in early 1985 he could not accept any possibility of a break up. He also became very jealous when he heard that she had been seen with other men and they frequently quarrelled about it. Their relationship became so bad that in August she left their home in Cromarty Road, Lordshill and they separated. Mitchell became so upset over this that the following November he decided to take drastic action.

He owned a shotgun and carefully sawed off the barrels and the stock to create a pistol-sized weapon. By this time his wife was living in a rented caravan in the garden of a house in Bassett Avenue.

The front of the house in Bassett Avenue.

At 5.30am on the morning of 8 November he went to the caravan and when his wife of 14 years opened the door he opened fire with the sawn-off shotgun, the force of the explosion throwing her back into the caravan. He then reloaded the gun, fired at her again as she lay on the floor, to ensure she was dead, and then turned the gun on himself, shooting himself in the head.

The woman occupier of the house heard the shots and raised the alarm via a '999' call. Det.Ch.Insp Keith Burton attended the scene, with Scenes of Crime officer DC Cliff Bull, and they were able to reconstruct what had taken place, confirming that nobody else was involved.

The subsequent inquest, on 3 December, resulted in a verdict of unlawful killing of Ann Harnden and suicide of Mitchell Harnden.

Both Ann and Mitchell Harnden were later cremated.

1985 – BETTY JONES – A VERY SPOILT AND VIOLENT NEPHEW

Reginald Parker, 44, a tenant in a block of flats at the junction of Howard and Atherley Roads, Shirley, allowed Raymond David Jones, 26, a friend he had met in prison, to use his flat while Reginald was in Southampton General Hospital undergoing major cardiac surgery.

On Thursday 19 September 1985 Reginald returned to his flat, helped by the flat manager, who also had a heart condition. When they entered the room they both experienced a terrible shock, finding a woman they did not know lying dead, obviously strangled, with a sash window cord around her neck. They staggered down the stairs and called the police, who on their arrival set up an immediate murder investigation as it was manifestly not a case of suicide.

The unfortunate Reginald Parker was initially detained by the police and questioned for several hours as a prime suspect, but when it was shown that the woman had been dead for some time, while he was in hospital, he was ruled out of the investigation. However, his former fellow prisoner, Raymond Jones, the only other person in possession of a key to the flat, was strongly suspected of being responsible. Jones was known to be violent.

The murder scene block of flats.

This suspicion was strengthened when it was confirmed that the dead woman was Raymond's aunt, Betty Jones, 48, a nurse of Longmynd Drive, Fareham. Raymond had formerly lived in nearby Foxbury Grove, Porchester, but had only just been released from Dartmoor and had nowhere to go, other than his friend's flat in Southampton. Betty's husband stated his wife had left their home at 8pm on the Wednesday as a result of Raymond phoning her and asking for help, requesting she visit him in Southampton. She failed to return and he reported her missing at 9am the following morning, the same day her body was found.

He said that his wife was a wonderful person who always tried to help Raymond, giving him money whenever he needed it and was the best friend he ever had. However, Raymond had been violently angry when he found that, because of her work and family commitments, she would not look after his children, who had been placed in care while he was in prison.

Raymond Jones was circulated as wanted for questioning and was arrested in Bordon three days later, after a fierce struggle. He readily admitted killing his aunt, saying he had become uncontrollably angry with her when she continued to refuse to look after his children. He was charged with her murder, appearing on remand in the magistrates' court handcuffed and with a badly bruised face and cut forehead, sustained when he resisted arrest at Bordon. He appeared at Winchester Crown Court on 10 June 1986, when he pleaded guilty to murder and was sentenced to life imprisonment.

1989 – JASON GREEN – A CITY CENTRE STABBING

A massive murder hunt, with a team of 30 detectives, was launched in the early hours of Saturday 16 September 1989, after blood-soaked Jason Spencer Green, 19, living in Darlington Gardens, Shirley, was found slumped and dying in the stairway of a multi-storey car park in Eastgate Street. He was rushed to Southampton General Hospital but all efforts

The Eastgate Street multi-storey car park.

to save him failed and he died from massive internal bleeding shortly after admission. Jason was subsequently cremated.

Enquiries revealed that six foot tall and blonde Jason had been involved in an earlier incident, at 1am that morning. Jason, with his friend Glen Marchant, had fallen out with Neil Robert May, 23, and his friend Christopher Rice in the nearby Raffles Nightclub. The dispute developed into a fight between the four and they were ejected from the club into Eastgate Street.

The fight continued outside, with the four of them entering the multi-storey car park. Jason knocked Christopher Rice to the ground and sat on top of him, punching him in the face. At the same time Jason's friend, Glen Marchant, ran away when Neil May produced a penknife and started slashing out at him.

Glen returned shortly afterwards and found Jason lying on the ground in the car park stairway, unconscious and in a pool of blood. There was no sign of May or Rice. An ambulance was called and the crew found that Jason had suffered three deep stab wounds in his back and several cuts on his face.

The ensuing police investigation caused an upset at the Raffles Nightclub the following Saturday night. The disco taking place was stopped two hours early when over 30 officers sealed the premises to question everybody inside as to their movements etc. the previous Saturday.

As each individual was questioned, with their identity verified, they were made to leave. Some initially refused to answer questions or establish their identity, until told they would be detained until such time as the police were satisfied.

As a result of enquiries made by the investigating team, both May and Rice were traced and arrested. May was arrested at his home, admitted the stabbing and said, 'I didn't realise how much damage a knife could do until the next morning when I heard the news'. May also said, 'My intention was to stop what was going on. I was dazed and scared.' He told the police that he had buried the knife and his bloodstained shirt in mud at Daisy Dip, Swaythling. He took officers to the site and both items were recovered.

Daisy Dip, Swaythling.

May said that after hitting Rice on the ground, Jason came towards him as though to also give him 'a good hiding'. He said he was drunk at the time he stabbed Jason 'on the spur of the moment' and was acting in self-defence as he thought he was about to be attacked.

He was charged with the murder and appeared before Mr Justice Ognall at Winchester Crown Court on Monday 24 September 1990, pleading not guilty.

In the course of the three-day trial May elected not to give evidence on his own behalf. His friend, Christopher Rice, although said to be a prosecution witness, also did not give evidence, although the reason for this was not given in court.

However, May's defending counsel, Christopher Leigh QC, said May felt as though he were already serving a life sentence and was thoroughly sorry. He would regret his actions for the rest of his life because he had acted impulsively, resulting in terrible consequences.

May was found not guilty of murder by the jury but convicted of manslaughter and sentenced to seven years imprisonment.

1990 – CLAIRE FORSHAW – A HALLOWEEN HORROR

Claire Forshaw, 23, was perfectly happy with her life, sharing a downstairs flat in a bedsit block in Rose Road, Portswood, with her boyfriend, Thomas William Legg, 32. The pair had travelled down from South Shields in late July 1990 and were described by a neighbour as 'a lovey-dovey couple'. Claire was a pretty girl, with very short blonde hair, punk style clothes, and usually wore a mini-skirt. Like Thomas, she was trying to overcome a drug problem. Thomas was also an alcoholic, brought

Thomas William Legg. (*Hampshire Constabulary History Society*)

about by the cot death of his daughter a year earlier, and the two coupled addictions meant he had severe behavioural problems.

Claire was told on 29 October 1990 that her father had died, so two days later she decided to pack her bags and return to her native South Shields. Thomas was unhappy about this and at 9am on 31 October, neighbours heard her screaming as the couple argued. The noise eventually died down and it was assumed that matters had been resolved.

However, Frank Tebano was looking after his parent's bed and breakfast business in Rose Road while they were on holiday and at midnight that Halloween night, went to check the two semi-detached properties. As he parked his car outside he noticed that the window of the ground floor bedsit No.16 was open, so he entered the house and went to the room, finding that the door was partially open. He knocked, and on receiving no answer entered the room and saw Claire lying on the floor with a pool of blood at the back of her head. Frank tried to find a pulse in her neck, without success, and found that the body was very cold. She had clearly been dead for some time. He called for both police and ambulance by '999' and on the arrival of the police they declared the area a crime scene.

Two blocks of modern flats, built on the site of the two former semi-detached houses in Rose Road.

Det.Supt Ray Piper took charge of the investigation and unemployed Thomas Legg was soon traced and questioned. He said he had returned to their room in Rose Road at 2am the previous day and found Claire in bed watching television. She said she was going back on drugs and he had replied, 'It's up to you, but if you are going back on drugs I have had enough. I don't want to know anything about it'. He had then got into bed with her, leaving the house at 8am. He added 'We have never been violent to each other. I never touched her and she never touched me'. When he returned late that night he found her dead on the floor, surrounded by syringes.

He then left the room and went to see friends at the Salvation Army Hostel in Oxford Street. He added, 'I didn't call the police because I had to have someone to talk to. I didn't know what was going on.' Det.Supt Piper was not satisfied with this explanation, especially because the dead girl's head wounds, with so much blood, made it obvious she had been attacked and his explanation for leaving the room without contacting the police was nonsensical. He was therefore charged with her murder.

He appeared before the Southampton magistrates the following day and was remanded in custody. While on remand in Winchester Prison he told probation officer John Blackmore that a Salvation Army captain at the Southampton Hostel had, for some time, talked to him about the Christian faith. He now realised he should take the matter seriously, so he had read the Bible in gaol and now decided he would not be able to lie on oath at his committal.

He then changed his story dramatically by telling the probation officer that he and Claire had had a violent row, after he woke at 7.30am, had some cider and smoked two joints. 'She grabbed a knife, long, like a bread knife. I was trying to get it off her. The next thing I know she was on the floor. I was at her feet, also on the floor. I can't remember how I got there. Claire was covered in blood, there was no heart beat.' He then placed the knife and his bloodstained clothes into a carrier bag, which he took with him and went for an all-day drinking binge at Hythe. The police were informed of this conversation.

Legg appeared before Mr Justice Cresswell at Winchester Crown Court on 21 January 1992 and pleaded 'not guilty' to murder.

Consultant pathologist Dr Roger Ainsworth told the jury that signs of suffocation, as well as stab wounds, were found on Claire Forshaw's bloodstained body. She had sustained three wounds to the back of the head, caused by a fairly heavy blunt instrument; as well as a stab wound in her abdomen and a smaller one on her left breast. He had seen a syringe and needles on the floor but no traces of a controlled drug had been found in her body.

Legg gave evidence on his own behalf, stating that he saw Claire with a knife in her hand, had a black-out and came round to find her covered in blood and dead. He stated he did not know whether he had killed her or not as he had black-outs several times a week and could never remember what had happened. He also told the court that he started drinking at the age of 18 and was addicted by the time he was 19.

His defence counsel, Mr James Wadesworth QC, urged the jury to return a verdict of manslaughter because Legg had either 'snapped' or was so drunk that he did not know what he was doing when he killed the girl. However, prosecuting counsel Mr David Thomas QC, said that somebody who is drunk can still form an intent. A drunken intent is not an excuse.

A medical report by Dr David Bennett was read to the court, in which he said he was unsure whether Legg's memory loss was genuine.

On 29 January after a week's trial and at the conclusion of the judge's summing up, the jury retired for just under three hours to return a verdict of guilty of manslaughter. Legg was then sentenced to five years imprisonment.

1990 – BRENDAN MICHAEL McSTAY – A GLUE-SNIFFING PATRICIDE

A noisy party at a block of apartments unwittingly sparked off a gruesome murder investigation. It was just before midnight on Friday 19 January 1990 when a '999' call to a disturbance outside a tower block in Ennerdale Road, Maybush, resulted in officers noticing an unusual bad smell coming from a first floor flat.

The block of flats in Ennerdale Road.

Getting no reply to knocking, they forced an entry and were surprised to find the decomposing body of 57-year-old Brendan Michael McStay, a french polisher, on a bed, covered with a duvet. On removing the duvet they were even more surprised to see that the bloodstained body was also covered by a picture of Jesus, placed symmetrically with the head of Jesus towards that of the body. There were also bloodstains on the wall and green mould on the body and on the pillow. A chisel and screwdriver, found in the flat, were removed for forensic examination.

Enquiries immediately focused on the victim's son, Thomas McStay, 18, who lived in the flat with his father. When officers searched the apartment after discovering the body, he was found barricaded in his room and had to be persuaded to come out. He was already under investigation for offences of arson, taking a vehicle without consent and indecent assault.

A subsequent post-mortem by Home Office pathologist Dr Roger Ainsworth revealed that Mr McStay had sustained over 55 stab wounds, mainly to the chest area. Death had occurred approximately a week earlier.

Detective Superintendent Ray Piper was in charge of the investigation as well as simultaneously investigating the Southampton murder of Ricky Haywood the previous October. (For an account of this murder see *Southampton Murder Victims*.)

When interviewed Thomas said he recalled having an argument with his father in the bedroom eight days earlier, after he had been asked to turn down the music volume on the television. The morning after he had woken up to find blood on his hands and thought he had been in a fight. He then walked into his father's bedroom and saw he was dead and covered in blood. He realised that he must have been responsible as he was alone in the house with the front door locked, but had no recollection as to what had happened.

Det.Con. Garth Lucas had found an empty tin of glue under Thomas McStay's mattress when he searched the flat and Thomas admitted, when questioned, that he

had been a glue sniffing addict since the age of 13. He had bought a half litre of glue to sniff a few days before his father's death, together with £10 worth of alcohol, and said he must have been hallucinating when the stabbings took place.

He was charged with his father's murder and appeared before Mr Justice Swinton Thomas at Winchester Crown Court on 3 November 1990, when he pleaded 'not guilty'.

In the course of the trial the Winchester Prison medical officer, Dr Anil Gupta, said that Thomas had told him he had been on the drug LSD on the evening his father had died, as well as having sniffed glue.

Thomas Peter McStay. (*Hampshire Constabulary History Society*)

Thomas gave evidence in his own defence, telling the court how glue sniffing made him hallucinate, with a buzzing noise in the head. He had once seen a tree crack open and the devil jump out.

He said that his father was continually 'having a go' at him for not working, and when he obtained work for him at Millbrook Furnishings, where he was also employed, he lost his job because of his glue sniffing habit.

Mr Guy Boney QC, defending Thomas, argued that he was under the influence of glue, drink and LSD at the time of the killing and was therefore guilty of manslaughter, not murder. But the jury returned a verdict of guilty and the judge sentenced McStay to life imprisonment, to be detained in a young offender's institution until he is 21, then moved to a prison.

Brendan McStay is buried in Hollybrook Cemetery in plot M17-113 and the headstone reads:

CHERISHED MEMORIES OF OUR
DEARLY
LOVED WIFE, MOTHER AND
NANNIE
DOROTHY MABEL MCSTAY
DIED 2-8-74 AGED 40 YEARS
WE LOVED YOU SO MUCH
GOD BLESS DARLING

BRENDAN MCSTAY
BELOVED HUSBAND, FATHER AND
GRANDAD
1932-1990

1994 – ANNE HOARE – A FALSE ALLEGATION OF AIDS

Anne Maria Susan Hoare, 28, a mother of four young children, was known to her neighbours in Cranbury Avenue as Roxanne Sandford, and was usually called Roxy. Her boyfriend, David Farrell, later said of her, 'She had a great sense of humour, took everything in her stride and would never hurt a fly. Her great concern was her children, never once did

Anne Hoare's home in Cranbury Avenue.

she lose her cool with them and gave them everything they wanted, even when she virtually had nothing.'

David had come into Anne's life after she had broken off a relationship with Derrick James Stanmore, 37, a Scotsman who now lived in the adjacent Denzil Avenue. She had fallen for Derrick in April 1994 when he visited her in a women's refuge on behalf of a prisoner in Winchester Prison she had been writing to.

Stanmore had also been in prison because, unknown to Anne, his previous relationship with a woman had ended violently when he drove a car through a wall outside her home. He had also been convicted in 1983 of threatening a woman with a replica firearm and striking her twice in the face.

Within a matter of weeks after Anne met him he was again sent to prison for a short spell for driving while disqualified, and on his release the pair moved to Southampton. However, Anne soon found that Stanmore was prone to violence, frequently striking her if they fell out over even a minor issue.

Matters came to a head in August when Stanmore found a form, in Anne's name, applying for an HIV test. When he questioned her she said she was worried because someone she had been involved with in the past might be HIV positive. He said this was the last straw in their affair and they split up. However, he remained very upset and told many of his friends of his fear that Anne had given him AIDS.

On the evening of Tuesday 18 October he met her outside her home and attacked her. A neighbour, hearing the commotion, came out and heard Stanmore shout that Anne was a bitch for giving him AIDS and that he was going to kill her. However, he was persuaded to stop and went away.

The following night he was seen carrying a knife at his home in Denzil Avenue by somebody visiting there, and was heard to say he was going to use it on 'Roxanne'. He said that instead of giving her a slapping the night before he should have cut her throat. He then left the house, saying he was going to visit Cranbury Avenue again.

The scene of the attack.

Anne's new boyfriend, David Farrell, heard a knock on the door at just after midnight and saw her leave the house. A few minutes later he heard a loud scream and ran out into the street where he saw Anne and Stanmore struggling together. As he ran towards them, Stanmore threw Anne towards him and ran off. David held onto Anne as she collapsed and he then saw that she was bleeding heavily from the front of her body. As he cradled her in his arms, on the pavement close to the junction with Frederick Street, neighbours called for an ambulance and it arrived, with the police, within 10 minutes.

Medical staff at the scene found she was bleeding profusely from multiple stab wounds to her body, but in spite of their efforts she was confirmed dead on arrival at the General Hospital. The immediate police reaction was to cordon off the area and detain David Farrell, but the true facts soon came to light and Stanmore was traced and arrested. A subsequent post mortem revealed that Anne had died of shock and haemorrhage from 16 stab wounds. It was also confirmed that she was HIV negative, not positive as alleged by Stanmore, who was charged with her murder.

He appeared before Mr Justice Ian Kennedy at Winchester Crown Court on 1 May 1995, when Stanmore's defending counsel Mr Stewart Jones, QC tried to argue that his client had been provoked and had only taken the knife either because he feared Anne's new boyfriend or intended to commit suicide. He said that if the jury believed he had been pushed beyond the limits of self control then the proper verdict should be manslaughter, not murder. He did not call Stanmore to give evidence on his own behalf.

Derrick Stanmore. (*Hampshire Constabulary History Society*)

Evidence was given of Stanmore's statements to the police while in custody. He had said he could not remember carrying out the fatal stabbing just yards from her home, could not remember having a knife in his hands or opening the knife, only recalled slapping and punching her. He told the police that he only wanted her to drop a proposed injunction against him, preventing him from seeing her, and to withdraw an assault charge. Mr Christopher Leigh QC, prosecuting, argued that the AIDS issue was a 'red herring' and that the stabbing was the act of a jealous bully.

At the end of the four-day trial the jury of seven women and five men, after four and a half hours deliberation, returned a unanimous verdict of guilty of murder, and the judge sentenced Stanmore to life imprisonment.

He said that Anne's killing 'was a cruel murder by Stanmore, who loved himself and whose actions had left four children without a mother'.

1995 – JAMES CLELAND – AN UNLUCKY WIN

51-year-old James Arthur Cleland, who lived in a flat in Neva Road, Midanbury, was an interesting character. A divorced man with two daughters, Sharmain and Sheree, he had lived in Canada for many years, with his Canadian father and English mother.

After the break up of his marriage to his wife Eileen he left to live with a tribe of North American Indians on a Canadian reservation but returned to England, where he was born, to look after his mother following the death of his father. She shared the flat with him in Neva Road but after she also passed away he took in a lodger.

Although generally regarded as a 'loner' he nevertheless enjoyed a drink with the locals, especially the Humble Plum in Bitterne but also the Bitterne Park Hotel. He

would talk of his days on the Indian reservation and how he lived and hunted with them. He also spoke of regretting the loss of contact with his children, keeping a photograph on his mantelpiece of them when they were young.

During the evening of Wednesday 25 January 1995, 'Canadian Jim', as he was

The Bitterne Park Hotel, Cobden Avenue.

generally known, because of his Canadian accent, went to the Bitterne Park Hotel, where he played the fruit machine.

He struck lucky with a large jackpot, happily cashing in his tokens at the bar. Jim then struck up a conversation with a stranger, Wayne David Sheppard, 22, who lived in a bedsit in Cobden Avenue, not far from the hotel. Sheppard had only just finished playing the fruit machine, losing his last few coins. The two men, realising they lived close to each other, decided at the end of the evening to walk home together. What then happened en route will never be fully known, but just after midnight a clearly distressed woman, Mandy Iden, made a '999' call to the police saying her boyfriend believed he might have killed a man in a fight in an alleyway off Cobden Avenue.

Officers, and an ambulance, went to the alleyway, where they found the body of Jim Cleland, under a laurel bush. He had severe head injuries and was certified dead at the scene. A murder investigation was immediately undertaken. An empty wallet, passport, documents and other items, identified as belonging to Cleland, were found on the ground near the body.

Mandy Iden's boyfriend was Wayne Sheppard and he had gone to their home in Cobden Avenue in a distressed state. He told her that after leaving the Bitterne Park Hotel Jim Cleland had attempted to kiss him, making a homosexual advance, and he had then attacked him.

She persuaded him to meet the police at a telephone kiosk near the alleyway, and when he did that he was arrested and taken to Bitterne police station.

Sheppard, a former boxer, repeated the story of being subject to a homosexual advance, saying he then 'lost his cool' after Cleland tried to kiss him, knocking him to

the ground in the alleyway and then stamping on his head. He said he then panicked when he could not find a pulse on the body so pulled it under a laurel bush before walking home to his girlfriend.

A subsequent post-mortem by pathologist Dr Roger Ainsworth, revealed that Cleland had suffered severe facial injuries, including a badly broken jaw, nose and both cheekbones.

Wayne Sheppard was charged with the murder and appeared before Mr Justice

The alleyway, leading from Cobden Avenue to Tamarisk Gardens.

Wayne Sheppard. (*Hampshire Constabulary History Society*)

Tucker at Winchester Crown Court, held at Bristol because of administrative problems, on Tuesday 4 July 1995. He pleaded 'not guilty' and during the course of the trial it was revealed that the deceased man was wearing women's underwear under his clothing.

The jury, by a 10-2 majority, took four hours to find Sheppard guilty of murder and his counsel, Christopher Leigh QC, said his client had considered suicide a number of times because he felt so guilty about what he had done.

The judge, in passing a sentence of life imprisonment, said, 'I am glad to hear you are so remorseful and feel proper responsibility for having caused that man's death.'

James Cleland is buried in unmarked plot P6-38 in South Stoneham Cemetery, together with photographs of his family, including a grandson, Connor James, of whom he knew nothing as his former wife had been trying to trace him to let him know he had become a grandfather.

1995 – FRANK DAVIS – MURDER OF A 'GAY LONER'

Francis Davis, 61, who came from the North and was known as Frank, came to the UK from Berlin during 1993 and took up residence in a flat above the Apollo Café & Takeaway in Bedford Place. He was known by his English friends as a flamboyant homosexual who dressed in army clothing and loved to pick up new sex partners.

The former Apollo Café, now very pleasant tea rooms under new ownership. The rear access to the first floor flat.

During the morning of Wednesday 26 July 1995, one of his friends, Tony Ling, who ran the café, realised that he had not seen Frank for some considerable time. Although the weather was sweltering hot, the upper flat windows were closed and he jokingly remarked to one of his customers, Mrs Peggy Bottomley that he did not want to go into the flat in case he found a body.

She was also Frank's friend and had not seen him for two weeks, so borrowed the key from Mr Ling and entered the flat. She went to the entrance of the living area, took two steps inside the door and saw Frank's naked decomposing body on the floor, lying on a silk dressing gown against the living room window. She immediately ran downstairs shouting out, 'Call the police, call the ambulance; there's a body up there, there's blood all over the place'.

When the police arrived it became clear that although there was no sign of a forced entry, there was evidence of some disturbance in the living room. The deceased was also bruised about the face and body and there were compression marks on the neck. The local press, when reporting the murder and after making their own enquiries, gave the headline 'Gay Loner murdered'.

Det.Supt Peter Long took charge of the investigation and a special incident room was set up in the police block in Hulse Road, with a 40-strong team of detectives. One of the apparently minor details found was a piece of paper in the victim's wallet bearing the name and address of a Denise Fearn in Bugle Street. Enquiries were made at that address to see if she could help build up a picture of Mr Davis's life, his associates etc.

However, she was not at home and enquiries were then made at the St Dismas Day Centre where, neighbours told the police, she often visited. They then discovered that 'she' was, in fact, a man, Dennis Fearn, 47, a cross-dresser who preferred to wear women's clothing. Unknown to the officers, Dennis became aware of their enquiries, panicked, withdrew all his money from his building society and travelled to Liverpool. He then went from hostel to hostel in Liverpool, Manchester and then Coventry, where he had relatives.

By now the police realised that he had fled the city and circulated him as wanted for questioning. He was eventually detained in a night shelter in Coventry and brought back to Southampton.

When questioned by Det.Sgt Tony Harris he said he had originally met Frank Davis at the Society of St Dismas and on 12 July 1995 they went to the flat in Bedford Place. Fearn said he was wearing women's underwear, tights, skirt, blouse and high heels at the time. They both carried on drinking vodka, heavily, until he passed out. When he came round he saw that Davis was dead, so panicked and left.

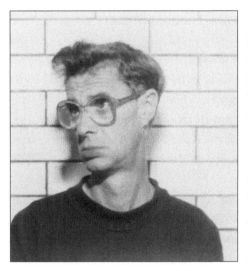

Dennis Fearn. (*Hampshire Constabulary History Society*)

Det.Sgt Harris suggested that Davis had made a homosexual advance on Fearn and for that reason had been attacked, but Fearn denied this. He said he was not gay but heterosexual, a woman in a man's body. He strongly denied murdering Frank Davis.

He was, however, charged with the murder and appeared before Mr Justice Tuckey at Winchester Crown Court on Monday 29 April 1996, when he pleaded 'not guilty' to murder but 'guilty' of manslaughter on grounds of provocation. This plea was not accepted by the prosecution. The unfortunate Francis Davis had, by then, been cremated.

The court was told that Fearn was receiving counselling for a sex-change operation. They also heard from his social worker, Alison Brooks, that she had a phone conversation with him while he was on remand in Winchester Prison. Fearn told her that Davis had tried to sexually assault him and that was why he had attacked him.

Mr Michael Vere-Hodge QC, for the prosecution, alleged that Fearn, after punching and kicking Davis, had tied something tight around his neck so that Davis could not breathe. He then placed a pillow over his face, washed his hands to remove the blood from them, and then removed Davis's clothes, taking them when he left the flat, to hinder any investigation. Davis was identified by his dental records and a post-mortem confirmed that death was due to asphyxiation, caused by compression of the neck and suffocation.

Fearn told the court that he had lost his temper when Davis tried to sexually assault him. He said it stirred memories of being abused as a boy by his grandfather and mother. He told the jury 'I just saw red. I thought, this is not going to happen to me again, so I hit him with my fist. I wanted to stop this picture in my mind of me and my mother. I was not thinking about Davis, he fell down, got up and I hit him again. He fell over and his head was near a belt. I put it round his neck and pulled, I am not sure how long it was. I did not intend to kill him, just to put him unconscious.'

The jury took four and a half hours, by a majority verdict of ten to two, to find Fearn guilty of murder. The judge said that life imprisonment was the only sentence the law allowed him to impose, and Fearn looked pale and agitated as he was sentenced.

1995 – SEAN MUSE – KILLED AFTER A 'GLASSING'

In July 1996 Michael Parroy QC, told the jury at Winchester Crown Court 'Mr Muse was clearly no angel. In the recent past it was clear that he could lose his self-control and become violent, but nothing he did justified what happened to him.'

The background to the trial was that at about 10.15pm on Thursday 17 August 1995 a fight had broken out in the car park outside the Bassett Social Club in Burgess Road. Trouble had started earlier inside the building, during a pool match with the Chamberlayne Arms, Sholing.

Unemployed kitchen worker Sean Muse, 28, of Belmont Road, had smashed a glass in the faces of Neil McKindoe and Gordon Thompson and had then been dragged outside by several customers, one of whom was Neil McKindoe's uncle, Darren Kenneth Stickland, 34, unemployed, of nearby Honeysuckle Road.

What then followed was initially confusing, but the end result was an unconscious Sean Muse being thrown into bushes at the side of the driveway leading up to the club. An ambulance crew treated him for half an hour before taking him to the General Hospital, where he underwent emergency surgery for severe head injuries.

The driveway leading to the redeveloped site of the former Bassett Social Club.

Sean was placed on a life support system, but in spite of all efforts his condition deteriorated and, with his family watching helplessly, he was declared brain dead and the machine switched off. The consequent murder investigation was now headed by Det.Supt Peter Long.

Sean Muse a 28-year-old man, living in a flat in Belmont Road, had spent most of his life in Swaythling, Southampton, attending Bassett Green First School and Bassett Juniors. His main interests had been listening to modern music, playing pool or cards with friends, and gambling on the horses. Although said to generally have a good nature he would often flare up in a temper and at the time of his death was awaiting a court hearing for assault.

He had previously been in prison after a fight, when he had been kicked in the head. On his discharge it was discovered that his brain had shrunk and he was placed on medication and never worked again. His weakened condition was such that he could easily be picked on and taunted, and his family suggested that this was why he had 'glassed' Neil McKindoe.

Immediately following the incident on 17 August 1995, a number of witnesses were interviewed, with a picture of what had happened slowly building up. Several individuals from the social club had dragged Sean outside, but the main participant in the subsequent attack was known to be Darren Stickland, 33, McKindoe's uncle. Stickland had a reputation in the area as a notorious 'hard man' who sympathised with the British National Party, flying the Union flag outside his Honeysuckle Road home.

One witness, Tina Smith, told the court she saw Stickland kick and stamp on Sean, saying, 'I am going to kill you'. Another witness, Amanda Plummer, said she saw Stickland and another man, Johnny Lambert, drag Sean out of the club and Stephen Blakely, the captain of the Chamberlayne Arms pool team said he witnessed the vicious attack.

Darren Stickland. (*Hampshire Constabulary History Society***)**

Darren Stickland pleaded 'not guilty' at his trial and denied having taken part in a revenge attack following the 'glassing' of his nephew. Following his arrest he told the police that Sean was a lifelong friend. He made a statement in which he said, 'He would have got a lynching if I had not got him out of there. He is my mate, I have known him longer than my nephew.' He also explained that he had left the scene before the arrival of the police because 'where I live hardly anyone talks to the police'.

He told the court that he was inside the Bassett Social Club checking his injured nephew when Sean was attacked and had played no part in it.

However, the jury were clearly influenced when told by Susan Jeffery, Stickland's former next door neighbour, that on the night of the attack she saw Stickland and his common-law wife Jackie, 31, dispose of his clothes. She had been woken at midnight by shouting and swearing and a gate banging shut. She then watched from her bedroom window as Stickland threw some jeans and a shirt into a car, which was driven off by Jackie.

The eight-day trial finished on 25 July, when the jury convicted Stickland of murder and Judge Martin Tucker QC, sentenced him to life imprisonment. Jackie was also convicted of disposing of Stickland's bloodstained clothing and was sentenced to 15 months, suspended for two years.

The unfortunate Sean Muse is buried in South Stoneham Cemetery, in plot D2-283 and the inscription reads:

TREASURED

MEMORIES OF A

DEAR SON & BROTHER

SEAN MUSE

BORN 26:5:67

TRAGICALLY TAKEN 19:8:95

AGE 28 YRS

SLEEP PEACEFULLY

With vase:

Forever In Our Thoughts

1996 – TERENCE, ALISON, NICOLA & PATRICK GOOD – BURNT TO DEATH

Former courier Frederick Lynn Hayworth, 59, of Eynham Avenue, Bitterne, blamed his wife's sister, Beverley Good, for the break up of his marriage to his wife Janette in 1995 and had become obsessed about it. Janette was a teenager when they married and was some 20 years younger. They had been married for almost 20 years but their divorce was now nearing completion.

She had been badly assaulted by her husband earlier that year, sustaining serious injuries, and went to live with her sister in Sullivan Road, Sholing. She later formed a relationship with another man, and Frederick became convinced that Beverley was partly responsible for his wife's alienation and believed that the failure of his marriage would affect their 14-year-old son, Paul. He also had four children from a previous marriage.

Frederick's obsession increased to the point where he felt he had to do something drastic, and on the night of Saturday 4 May 1996 he put his plan into action. He had been further upset because a few months earlier Mrs Good had informed the social services that Frederick had been cheating on benefits.

In the early hours of Sunday 5 May, after returning home from a dinner dance in Botley where he had been drinking, he took a can of petrol from his garden shed and cycled with it to the Good family's semi-detached council house in Sullivan Road; with terrible consequences.

Kelly Good, 14, was watching a late night film in her bedroom when she heard the sound of what turned out to be petrol, being poured through the front door letterbox. She opened her bedroom door and saw flames at the bottom of the stairs. She ran into her parent's bedroom to wake them, and they joined her on top of the landing. As they did so a huge ball of flame shot up the stairs.

Kelly looked out of the window and saw a man hurrying away from the house, pushing a mountain bike. She then got into bed with her brother, Patrick Thomas Good, 7, and pulled the duvet over them to overcome the smoke. When she heard her mother calling for help from her bedroom window she ran to join her, but Mrs Good had already climbed out of the window to escape the flames. Kelly also leapt from the window, landing on the conservatory below, after having badly burnt her arms on the flaming curtains.

By then Mervyn Good had battled through the flames in a vain attempt to find his fire extinguisher, but was forced to escape through a back door. He tried to climb up the conservatory, to rescue his other four children, Terence Christopher, 13; Alison Fay, 10; Nicola Ann, 8; and Patrick Thomas, 7; but found it impossible. Both parents had to be held back by neighbours as they tried to enter the house that was engulfed in flames.

Around 20 firefighters from the Hightown and St Mary's stations soon arrived on the scene but the fire had taken a very strong hold, with 20 foot high flames engulfing the house. The intense heat had buckled the building's metal staircase, shattered the windows and ruptured a gas main. A wall of flame shot into the face of fire-fighter Dave Brewer when he broke a window in an attempt to gain entry and when firefighter Paul Cambell tried to fight his way up the stairs to find the children, he was constantly beaten back by the flames.

He later said 'We tried two or three times to get in but had to keep running back out again because it was just too hot; the flames were raging and my gloves were steaming. By the time we found the children the fire was under control but there was nothing we could do for them. There is just no way they could have survived.'

Sadly, the bodies of the four children were found by the firefighters at the back of a first floor bedroom. The blaze, which destroyed almost every room in the house, left four fire-fighters needing hospital treatment for burns and it was estimated that the smoke, heat and flames had reached temperatures of around 1,000 degrees centigrade. The building and adjoining semi-detached house were subsequently demolished.

The police had arrived simultaneously with the fire-fighters and within hours Frederick Heyworth had been arrested by DC Sommers and DC Boyle. He said he had

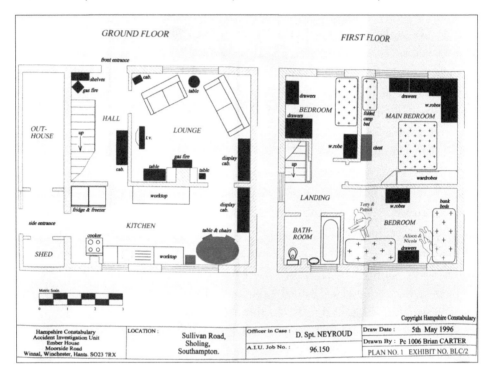

Top: Plan of the house in Sullivan Road, showing the location of the children's bodies. Drawn by PC Brian Carter. (*Hampshire Constabulary History Society*)

Left: New houses on the site of the former Good family home.

not been to the house in Sullivan Road for more than a year and said that being accused of starting the fire was nonsense. He was nevertheless detained while the police made further enquiries, being compelled to obtain a magistrate's order to hold him without charge, the maximum permissible time being 96 hours.

Apart from the evidence of young Kelly Good, who had been taken to hospital by ambulance and later transferred to Odstock Hospital near Salisbury, a further witness was traced. He was ambulance co-ordinator David Watts, who had attended the scene.

He said that after leaving Sullivan Road he drove along South-East Road, at a point known as 'Muddy Bottom', when he saw a bicycle lying on the pathway between the grass and the fence. He stopped, as he thought there might have been an accident, and saw Frederick Heyworth.

He asked 'Are you OK mate?' and got the reply 'Yes' and something about the bike having broken down. Heyworth kept in the shadows, with his back to Mr Watts, and only turned his head to answer.

A search was made of the area and PC Hewes found a green petrol can on the side of Botley Road and PC Fahy found a black holdall some distance away. A search of Heyworth's home in Eynham Avenue resulted in DC Whitcher recovering identical green and red petrol cans from the garden shed. The three petrol cans had similar handwriting on them and a forensic handwriting expert, Michael Hall, stated they were all in the same handwriting. The black holdall was also identified by family members as belonging to Frederick Heyworth.

The police continued to question Heyworth, who persisted in denying everything, but after he was seen by his solicitor, who told him some of the police case against him, he was later found in his cell with head injuries and taken to hospital. When he was fit to be interviewed by DC Sommers and DC Boyle three days later he stated, 'I must have had petrol because I remember putting it through the front door. I must have ignited it. The next thing I remember is waking up at ten to seven answering a call from a family member telling me about the fire.'

He also said, 'I thought they were away for the bank holiday, I just wanted to pay them back. Why should they be enjoying themselves on a weekend when I'm working 14 hours a day trying to keep a family and home together and my wife's just got a posh flat? I just know in my own heart that I never intended to kill those children.'

Disproving his statement was the fact that at the time of the fire the bathroom light was on, visible from outside, and, most important, the family's Ford Escort car was parked outside, showing they could not have been on holiday, as he alleged he thought. He also failed to check the fact by knocking on the door or phoning them.

Frederick Heyworth. (*Hampshire Constabulary History Society*)

He was charged with the murder and appeared before Mrs Justice Steel at Winchester Crown Court in May 1997, when he pleaded 'not guilty' to four charges of murder. The four unfortunate children had, by then, been cremated.

In the course of the trial Heyworth claimed he had no real memory of setting fire to the petrol, but admitted having put it through the letter box. The jury took seven hours to find him guilty of the four murders and Mrs Justice Steel, when she sentenced him to four life sentences, plus 10 years concurrent for the attempted murder of Kelly, Mervyn and Beverley Good, said,

'On May 5 last year you committed an act of the greatest wickedness. What evil brainstorm prompted you to act as you did, we shall never know. Unhappiness, jealousy, anger, revenge – all these were disclosed by the evidence. Mercifully, the evidence shows the children died from fumes, rather than flames. That is the only crumb of comfort which can be salvaged from the horror of the fire you caused.'

1996 – TRACY SELF – A KNIFE HORROR ATTACK

Tracy Self, 36, was devoted to her two children, aged 11 and seven, and lived in a ground floor flat in Cheviot Road, Millbrook. She was said by her neighbours to be charming and friendly, and would always stop for a chat.

She met Bernard Finlay, 26, a black man, in 1995 and by the summer of 1996 he had moved in with her. Unknown to her he had three previous convictions; in 1991 for wounding with intent and 1994 for threatening police with a knife after rowing with a girlfriend. He was on probation for assaulting another girlfriend and was due to attend an anger management course in September 1996.

During the evening of Saturday 7 September, she went to a nightclub in

The ground floor flat in Cheviot Road.

Bernard Finlay. (*Hampshire Constabulary History Society*)

Southampton, in the course of which she took some ecstasy and amphetamines and returned home at about 2am. A row then broke out between them when he questioned her about who she had been out with that evening. She then told him to pack his bags and move out the next day. Her 16 and 14-year-old nephews were in the living room at the time and saw Finlay lose his temper, rip off his T-shirt, shout and swear, smash a glass cabinet, break up the handrails on the staircase and then threaten their aunt with a piece of wood.

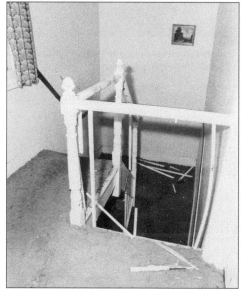

Smashed handrails on the staircase. (*Hampshire Constabulary History Society*)

She told them to leave the room and as they did so one of them looked back and saw him grab a handful of knives from the kitchen, return and start to stab their aunt, before rushing out of the building.

The nephew then phoned the police from the house and when they arrived they found a truly horrific scene. The living room ceiling and walls were splattered with blood, with Tracy's body on the floor, clearly dead. A meat cleaver was found, apparently used to cut off a hand, and there was a terrible stab wound in the head.

As a result of what the police were told the surrounding district was searched to trace Finlay, and he was located 40 minutes later in the Regents Park area and detained.

Smashed interior door and heavy bloodstains on the open entrance door. (*Hampshire Constabulary History Society*)

He was charged with her murder and appeared before Mr Justice Ian Kennedy at Winchester Crown Court in July 1997.

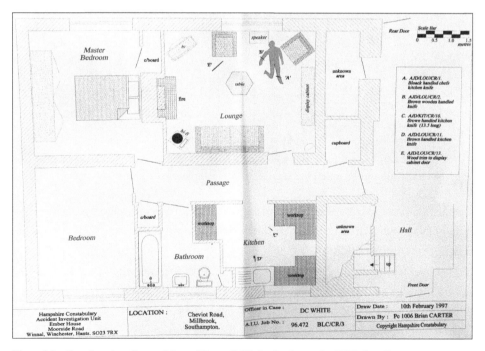

Plan of the flat, showing the position of Tracy Self's body, drawn by PC Brian Carter. (*Hampshire Constabulary History Society*)

Dr Roger Ainsworth, pathologist, told the court that Ms Self had been stabbed five times, one made in the head with such force as to pierce her brain, with the tip of the knife bent almost double. He also found that she had taken a quantity of amphetamines and ecstasy consistent with heavy substance abuse.

Finlay told the court that he had taken ecstasy and smoked cannabis that evening and had accepted that the relationship was over. He stated he was not upset when he was asked to leave but admitted losing control when Tracy made racial taunts about his black colour, calling him a black bastard.

Through his counsel he denied murder but admitted manslaughter on the grounds of provocation. This was not accepted by the prosecution and at the conclusion of the evidence the jury returned a verdict of 'guilty of murder'. The judge then sentenced him to life imprisonment.

Tracy Self is buried in plot 9/293 in Millbrook Church graveyard.

The inscription reads:
TRACY JANE SELF
MUM
BORN 10TH OCTOBER 1960
DIED 8TH SEPTEMBER 1996

IT BROKE OUR HEARTS TO LOSE YOU
YOUR (SIC) MISSED BY EVERYONE
TOO LOVED TO BE FORGOTTEN
YOU WERE THE GREATEST MUM

1996 – ROBIN STODDART – THE CONSEQUENCES OF DRINK

Robin John Stoddart, 40, better known as Johnny Rivers, particularly to his drinking companions, was unemployed and had a flat in Derby Road, which he shared with Stephen Cree.

At about 10pm on Sunday 21 January 1996, he took a taxi from his home in Derby Road and joined his friends Susan Freeman, Joseph Bolton and Samuel McKinley, 35, in a flat over a shop in Onslow Road.

McKinley lived in a flat in Howard Road, Shirley, some distance away.

The Derby Road premises.

The four of them had already indulged in heavy drinking the previous day and this was a continuation of their drinking session.

What took place during the heavy bout of drinking is unclear, as all the participants were extremely drunk, but what is clear is that a fierce argument broke out between Robin Stoddart and Samuel McKinley. In the course of this, at around 2am, McKinley became very aggressive and started to wave a knife around saying, 'I could slit your throat anytime', while waving it under Stoddart's face.

Stoddart then gave a loud scream as the knife was suddenly thrust into his right thigh, which bled profusely as his femoral artery was severed. The others in the room could see the knife sticking in his thigh, with the blood furiously pumping out of his leg. McKinley removed the knife and ran away from the flat, carrying the knife, together with another one, and kicked them both under a car as he ran along nearby Lyon Street.

Those remaining called for an ambulance, but when it arrived the crew found that Stoddart was dead, lying in a pool of blood. The police also attended and detained Susan Freeman and Joseph Bolton on suspicion of being involved in the death, but then, as a result of what they said, traced McKinley, naked in bed, to Stoddart's house in Derby Road.

Stephen Cree said that McKinley had been with him all night, but both men were detained on suspicion of murder and taken to Lyndhurst police station. Cree then admitted that McKinley had suddenly turned up in Derby Road and asked him to say that he'd been there all night. Cree was then released. Susan Freeman and Joseph Bolton, when questioned, stated they had seen McKinley fighting with Stoddart, who had then collapsed, bleeding heavily.

McKinley was interviewed in the afternoon of Monday 22 January, in the presence of his solicitor, Mr Knight. He admitted going to the Onslow Road flat with Stoddart and sitting with him on the sofa, watching TV and drinking. He said that he didn't actually recall stabbing Stoddart but did remember sitting on the sofa next to him with the knife in his hand and seeing blood pouring from Stoddart's leg.

He also readily admitted that he had run away and told the police where he had thrown the knives, which they recovered. He said he had drunk about seven litres of cider and could not remember much of what had happened, other than seeing blood coming from the leg and two knives in his hand.

McKinley was charged with the murder and appeared before Mr Justice Ian Kennedy on Tuesday 29 October 1996. During the three-day trial he admitted having attacked Stoddart but said he had no recollection of stabbing him. He said, 'I remember seeing blood but I don't know where it came from. Then I remember seeing a knife in my hand. I didn't know there was a knife in my hand and saw blood but I didn't see any injury. It was, like, confusion at the time. I remember running, trying to get away.'

The unfortunate Robin Stoddart, alias 'Johnny Rivers', had by then been cremated.

Top left: The flat above the shop in Onslow Road where the attack took place. (*Hampshire Constabulary History Society*)

Top right: Samuel McKinley. (*Hampshire Constabulary History Society*)

Bottom: Interior views of the room, showing blood on the floor. (*Hampshire Constabulary History Society*)

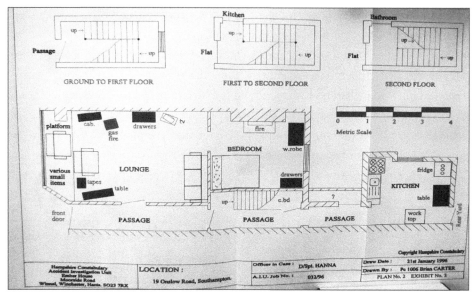

Plan, drawn by PC Brian Carter, showing the plan of the murder scene. (*Hampshire Constabulary History Society*)

McKinley's defence put forward an argument that he was too drunk to form any intent to murder, but after an hour and half the jury decided that he was, in fact, guilty of murder.

The judge said, 'There is no purpose in preaching to you or people like you about alcohol. A man is dead because of excessive consumption of alcohol and he is dead at your hand and you must pay the price.' He then sentenced McKinley to life imprisonment.

1998 – DAVID PAYNE – HORRIFIC STABBINGS AND STAMPINGS

Former merchant seaman and unemployed David Richard Payne, 54, had lived alone in a bedsit in Derby Road for 10 years, during which time he only received one visit from either family or friends. He was diabetic and a heavy drinker, in the habit of brandishing a knife if he felt threatened by other residents, but was otherwise a rather lonely, sad and pathetic figure.

During the evening of Sunday 26 October 1998, Edward Smith, another resident in the bedsit, found Payne's door

David Payne. (*Hampshire Constabulary History Society*)

open and saw him lying on the floor of his room, covered in blood and naked from the waist down. He was unconscious but breathing shallowly.

Edward Smith then saw another resident, William Smith, 20, with Steven Martin Blumberg, 28, who lived in nearby Nichols Road, as they were both leaving the bedsit. They said they had attacked David Payne but left when they heard Edward Smith calling the emergency services.

Payne was taken to the General Hospital and the police were called. They immediately sealed off the area, including the adjacent Graham Road, and within a few hours had traced and arrested William Smith and Steven Blumberg at the Nichols Road address. William Smith initially admitted that he and Blumberg had attacked Payne, because Payne had threatened them with a knife, but Blumberg remained silent throughout his individual questioning.

During his questioning Smith said, 'No one holds a knife to me and gets away with it', and showing his injured hand to another officer, said, 'You wouldn't think I was squeamish after having stabbed a man half to death!'

The bedsit in Derby Road.

Both men were detained and it was discovered that Payne had suffered appalling injuries. He had sustained multiple stab wounds to his forehead, shoulder, neck, throat and chest and these were linked to a knife, fork and screwdriver found in the flat. He also had severe head and chest injuries, consistent with having been kicked and stamped on. There was also some evidence that scalding water had been poured over his bare buttocks and thighs.

Both men were charged with causing grievous bodily harm and remanded in custody to Winchester Prison. While there, on remand, Blumberg laughed as he boasted to fellow inmates of how he and Smith had attacked David Payne. He said he had stabbed him 33 times with a screwdriver and then, jumping up and down, laughing, showed how they had jumped on his head.

Fellow inmate Michael Dorward secretly taped another 15-minute conversation with Blumberg, in which he described how David Payne was battered, kicked, punched and stamped on and stabbed with a breadknife, two-pronged fork and screwdriver.

Blumberg said he stabbed Payne 64 times and Will Smith had repeatedly kicked and stamped on him.

On the evening of Saturday 2 November, David Payne, who had undergone emergency surgery on his admission and placed on a life-support machine, deteriorated and died. A post-mortem revealed that as well as the stabbing and scalding wounds, he had suffered 14 broken ribs, a fractured bone in his forehead and a stab wound to his neck that had fractured his voice box. He had even been repeatedly stabbed with the needle of the syringe used to treat his diabetes. He was subsequently cremated.

The charges were now amended to that of murder and both men appeared before Mr Justice Tucker at Winchester Crown Court on 5 October 1999.

During the trial it emerged that the two men had gone to David Payne's room after they had burgled the St Dismas detox unit, during which Smith cut his hand on a broken pane of glass. They asked Payne for the taxi fare so Smith could go to the General Hospital for treatment, and when he refused, holding a knife up, they attacked him.

Smith alleged that Blumberg had 'gone mad', laying into him with a knife and fork. He said that it was Blumberg who stamped on his head several times and cut his throat with broken glass from a picture frame.

On the other hand, Blumberg told the jury that they had panicked when Payne said he was going to stab them if they didn't 'get the hell out of my room' and Smith started punching him on the side of the head. Payne fell to the floor, dropping the knife. Blumberg said, 'I then picked up the nearest thing to me, a cross-topped screwdriver and started to attack Mr Payne with it in the upper chest. I had no intention of killing him. It was more like a prodding movement than a stabbing.'

Mr Nigel Pascoe QC, defending Smith, told the jury that at the time of the attack Smith was suffering an 'abnormality of the mind' that was supported by two psychiatric reports and he sought a reduced charge of manslaughter. Mr Guy Boney QC, defending Blumberg, said that his client did not inflict the injuries that caused Payne's death; these were carried out by Smith.

William Smith – Steven Martin Blumberg. (*Hampshire Constabulary History Society*)

The 15-minute taped conversation in Winchester Prison was played to the jury and the judge asked Dr Ainsworth how much force would be required to crush Payne's ribs. He answered, 'He had strong ribs and it would take considerable force, a heavy stamp'.

The jury returned a verdict of murder against both the accused, and the judge told them, 'The jury have convicted you both of a savage, sustained, cruel and degrading attack. The victim was an inoffensive and middle-aged man in his own room at night. This case has provided an extreme example of the mindless violence with which courts have to deal.' He then sentenced them both to life imprisonment.

1999 – PATRICK COSGROVE – A DRUNKEN FRATRICIDE?

Patrick Thomas Cosgrove, 38, and his older brother, scaffolder Kevin John, 46, enjoyed a day of heavy drinking in Shirley on Friday 26 March 1999, before returning to Kevin's ground floor flat at Clover Nook, Old Redbridge Road.

Clover Nook, in Old Redbridge Road.

They had spent some time in the Henry Paget public house in Anglesea Road before buying a bottle of wine at a local store, and were pretty drunk by the time they had consumed it at home. It was widely assumed that a violent quarrel broke out between the two, as the noise of shouting and thuds was heard by their neighbours, before everything went quiet.

It was not until 9.50am the following morning that the fatal consequence of their assumed argument came to light, when Kevin made an emergency call saying, 'I think

Patrick Cosgrove. (*Hampshire Constabulary History Society*)

my brother is dead, he's brought up blood'. Paramedics attended and found Patrick deeply unconscious, with blood on his face originating from his nose.

He was taken to hospital and Kevin told the police, who had also attended, that his brother had a drink problem and had suffered a spontaneous nose bleed while they were dancing to rock music. He said that when he went to bed his brother was still awake and denied there had been any disagreement between them. When he woke the following morning he found Patrick lying face up on the sofa, with no sign of life. He attempted to resuscitate him and then dialled 999.

Despite medical attention Patrick died the following day in the General Hospital. The cause was found to be an internal haemorrhage, with blood entering his brain as a result of a broken nose, but when the police consequently called at Clover Nook there was no sign of Kevin.

Enquiries were made to trace him but without success, until he phoned the police 20 days later, on 17 May, and agreed to return for interview at Southampton Central Police Station.

He then told them after his brother had been taken to hospital he had drawn the bulk of his savings, £135, from his account and travelled to Bournemouth, where he rented a room under an assumed name. When he had no further money he went to a night shelter and also slept under Bournemouth pier. He said, 'I'm sorry I haven't been in before, I've been a bit disorientated'.

Kevin was arrested and charged with murdering his brother, appearing at Winchester Crown Court before Mr Justice George Newman on Tuesday 1 February 2000. The prosecution case was that Kevin had struck his brother in the face with such force as to break his nose but failed to send for medical attention until the following morning. Two clumps of Patrick's hair, in two separate places, had been found on the floor of the flat, indicating a fight.

Pathologist Dr Roger Ainsworth gave evidence that Patrick's broken nose was consistent with being punched, but when cross-examined by defending counsel, Christopher Leigh QC, he had to admit that it was also consistent with Patrick falling on his face. The judge later instructed the jury to return a 'not guilty' verdict to murder on the grounds that post-mortem evidence had failed to prove Kevin had intended to cause serious bodily harm. The charge was then reduced to that of manslaughter.

However, Michael Vere-Hodge QC, prosecuting, in his closing address pointed out that two clumps of Patrick's hair had been found in the flat and said 'You don't have clumps of hair pulled out for no reason. It is not suggested the man pulled his own hair out.' But Christopher Leigh, in his closing address, to the jury said, 'The Crown say there is no explanation from the defence about the hair. I turn the question around, as I am entitled to do, and ask 'have the prosecution explained how it happened so you are sure?'

Kevin had given evidence on his own behalf, telling the court he had disappeared because he could not face his family. A friend had told him of his brother's death in hospital and he then felt 'lost and empty, I was just walking around in a trance'. He denied that any argument had taken place, the sounds of shouting and banging heard by the neighbours were him trying to stop Patrick from returning to his hostel accommodation in a drunken state. He confirmed his earlier statement to the police, that he had not seen any injury to Patrick until he found him lifeless on the sofa the following morning, when he immediately called the ambulance. He had only left Southampton because he panicked and did not want to face his family.

At the conclusion of the week-long trial the jury of seven women and five men retired for three hours and on their return gave a unanimous verdict of 'not guilty' of manslaughter and Kevin Cosgrove was discharged.

He afterwards, accompanied by members of his family, told the *Southern Daily Echo* crime reporter Ian Pope, 'Now is the first time we can grieve. I just want to spend time with my family and relax.' He also attacked the police for refusing to allow him to attend his brother's funeral while he was on remand.

1999 – SHAUN FITZPATRICK – A STREET STABBING

It all started at around 2.20am on Saturday 4 December 1999, when Patrick Michael D'Arcy, 17, of York Close, Northam, 'flew into a rage' when the kitchen window of his cousin's flat in Exford Drive, Harefield, was shattered. Pieces of glass had fallen onto his cousin's young baby who was asleep in the room.

Patrick D'Arcy had earlier traded insults with a group of drunken teenagers on a landing inside the block of flats and the smashed window was the outcome. He ran out of the flat onto the landing, having first grabbed a large kitchen knife, and the group of about seven youths scattered, some almost falling down the stairs, as they tried to escape the enraged Patrick brandishing the knife.

He was shouting and screaming, at one stage tearing off his shirt in temper, as he chased them out of the block into Exford Drive. One of the youths, 18-year-old Shaun

The block of flats, now derelict and awaiting demolition. The flat concerned is at the extreme right of the third floor.

Stephen Fitzpatrick, who lived with his parents in nearby Somerton Avenue, picked up a long piece of wood and broke it in half, giving one half to another of the youths. His piece was around two or three feet long and he started to walk back towards the flats, saying, 'Let's go and get him'. His friend, however, dropped his piece of wood as he was frightened of the knife they could see carried by D'Arcy.

Shaun was clearly unafraid but as the two met in the roadway the youths saw Shaun fall to the ground. D'Arcy then left the scene and when the others went to Shaun's aid they saw he was clearly badly hurt, bleeding from his chest.

An ambulance and police were called and Shaun was taken by paramedics to the General Hospital, where he died an hour later. A later post-mortem revealed he had sustained a stabbing wound that had penetrated his chest to a depth of four inches and severed his pulmonary artery, resulting in uncontrolled bleeding and his consequent death.

Exford Drive had become a murder scene and was sealed off, allowing scenes of crime officers to carry out a detailed examination. The investigation, with the code name Operation Hermitage, was headed by Det.Supt John James, whose team of 20 detectives carried out house-to-house enquiries in the area.

Shaun, a former pupil at Woodlands Community School, had only recently started as a labourer at the new West Quay shopping complex, and was popular among his peers in the area. As a result tributes began pouring in and signed flags, candles and flowers were placed along the fence near where he collapsed.

The end of Exford Drive, the scene of the stabbing.

D'Arcy, who had spent the night in his cousin's flat, was woken at 7am that morning by a phone call from a friend telling him to switch on the radio. He then heard that Shaun had died. He later went to Bitterne police station where he admitted the stabbing but said it was in self-defence and that he had only intended to scare Shaun. He stated that on hearing the news of the death 'The shock was just unreal. He was all right, he walked away. I never thought that I had killed him. At that stage I thought it couldn't be true. I was scared, shocked. It was just like a bad dream. I couldn't believe it because there was no blood.'

His interview was taped, in the course of which he said, sobbing throughout, 'It looked like he was going to swing the piece of wood at me. He had it above his head. I intended just to pop his puffer jacket before he went to swing at me. I just basically wanted to scare him. He backed off and laughed. I saw feathers coming out of his jacket. He started backing away from me and I saw my chance to get away before the rest of the boys came back for me. There was no blood on the knife, no blood whatsoever. I thought I had done the deed.'

D'Arcy was charged with murder and appeared before Mr Justice Turner at Winchester Crown Court on 3 July 2000, when he pleaded 'not guilty'.

During the course of the trial the jury heard the taped interviews with the police and were shown how he had demonstrated to the police the classic downward movement of the knife, enabling it to penetrate Shaun's chest. D'Arcy also gave evidence on his own behalf, saying he had laughed after the incident, not realising he had caused a fatal injury.

He told the jury, 'I thought I would scare him. I wanted to stop him from chasing me so I could get away. I got to Shaun and he said "Come on D'Arcy; give me what you've

Patrick D'Arcy. (*Hampshire Constabulary History Society*)

got." I got scared, stabbed out and popped his puffer jacket. I saw feathers come out of his jacket and he laughed at me and then started backing off. I felt scared and thought I had to scare him. I just stabbed out straight with my fist.'

On Tuesday 11 July 2000, at the end of the six-day trial, the jury returned a verdict of not guilty of murder but guilty of manslaughter on the grounds he had been provoked by Shaun confronting him with a piece of wood.

Mr Justice Turner said, 'One victim dead is the result of your intention either to kill or, I prefer to think, to cause Shaun Fitzpatrick serious physical harm with a kitchen knife of some length. The jury has understandably concluded that you were provoked. That you intended Shaun Fitzpatrick harm is without doubt. I sentence you to eight years youth custody.'

A tree was planted by relatives and friends in his memory and is opposite the scene of the fatal attack. (It can be seen just above the street name plate of Exford Drive in the earlier photograph.) The plaque on it reads:

In Loving Memory of a Special Son.
It's sometimes hard to know, Why
some things happen as they do
For so much joy and happiness, Was
centred around you
It seems so hard to comprehend,
That you're no longer here
But all the happy memories, Will
help to keep you near
You're thought about with pride
Son, With each mention of your
name
Death cannot change a single thing,
The love will still remain

Shaun is buried in St Mary Extra Cemetery, in plot H47-198, and the inscription reads:

IN LOVING MEMORY OF

SHAUN STEPHEN

FITZPATRICK

A VERY MUCH LOVED SON AND BROTHER
WHO WAS TRAGICALLY TAKEN FROM US ON
4TH DECEMBER 1999 AGED 18 YEARS

GONE IS THE FACE WE LOVED SO DEAR,
SILENT THE VOICE WE LOVED TO HEAR.
IT BROKE OUR HEARTS TO LOSE YOU,
BUT YOU DID NOT GO ALONE
FOR PART OF US WENT WITH YOU,
THE DAY GOD CALLED YOU HOME.
WE MISS YOU SHAUN
ALWAYS IN OUR THOUGHTS, FOREVER IN
OUR HEARTS
GOD BLESS
LOVE FROM YOUR BROKEN-HEARTED
FAMILY
MUM, DAD, JAMIE, BONNIE, BRADLEY
XXXXX

Shaun Stephen Fitzpatrick (as depicted on his
headstone).

2000 – REZIA BEGUM – MURDER IN A TAKEAWAY

Rezia Begum 41, was born in East Pakistan, now Bangladesh, and when she was about 15 years of age married Khalilur Rahman, 45, also born in Bangladesh. They moved to England and lived in the Birmingham area for 10 years, before returning to Bangladesh for around eight months. In accordance with their religion, Rezia kept her maiden name.

They then returned to England, initially living in Swindon before moving to Southampton in 1991, moving into their family home in Burgess Road in 1998. By then they had six children, whose ages ranged from three to 21 and had both worked in various Indian restaurants and takeaway shops in the UK. Rahman spoke both Bengali

The family home.

and English but his wife could only speak her native Bengali.

In 1998 Rahman bought the lease to the takeaway premises of what was then known as Kingsland Kebabs in St Mary Street. He extended the business to include both Indian style and other takeaway foods, such as burgers and chips, changing the name to The Shalimar Tandooris and Kingsland Kebabs. It was also the first Indian restaurant in Southampton to take orders through the Internet. There was a flat above the premises but this was not used as living accommodation.

The premises had a small public area at the front, with a serving counter, and the rear used for food preparation and store. A basement contained chest freezers, a computer, sofa and table, and was used as an office. The front of the shop had the windows covered with grilles and a detachable centre section secured by two padlocks. It was open seven days a week from 5pm to 2am.

Rahman's three eldest sons would help in the shop when they finished school, college or work, and his wife Rezia would also be at the shop most days, around lunchtime, to clean up from the previous night's business. Once her sons arrived she would usually return home, around 6pm, with her other younger children.

Rezia Begum was deeply religious, observing the Muslim faith and praying daily according to the Koran, also observing all the religious festivals. On the other hand, Rahman was not a practising Muslim and did not attend the local mosque.

When their four older children were later questioned by the police, they all described their father as being violent towards his wife and the older boys. He was said to have a particularly violent temper when drunk and appeared to have a drink problem. He also discussed with the family his wish to go on a pilgrimage to Saudi Arabia so that his wife 'could cleanse her sins'. Rezia strongly denied that she had sins and did not need to go, and this angered him.

The former Shalimar Tandooris and Kingsland Kebabs in 2012. Still an Indian takeaway but with a new name and owners.

What became particularly disturbing towards the end of 1999 was that Rahman became obsessed with the notion that his wife was having an affair. He was paranoid in the belief that a man came to the family home at midnight, leaving before Rahman and his sons returned after 2am. It was this belief that brought about his unusual action on Saturday 15 January 2000, their busiest night, when he closed the shop at midnight instead of 2am and returned home. Everything at home was, of course, perfectly normal.

The following day, in front of his sons, he accused his wife of ruining the family by giving money to her family in Bangladesh and making expensive telephone calls to them, again accusing her of having an affair.

That same day, Amirlin Nessa, a close friend of Rezia, spoke to her on the phone. Rezia told her there had been arguments with her husband over her and her sons' refusal to go to Bangladesh and the older ones agreeing to the arranged marriages Rahman said he was going to make. It was then agreed that she would meet Rezia on Saturday 22 January to discuss the family problems.

A further argument occurred on Wednesday 19 January when Rahman said he had proof of an affair because he had found a Benson & Hedges cigarette butt at the house and he only smoked Rothmans. His son Abul then told him that the butt belonged to his uncle's father who had visited the house the previous day, but this did not pacify Rahman.

That same evening Rahman unexpectedly returned home at 7.30pm, and rushed around the house collecting documents, passports and birth certificates, placing them in a green bag. His son Kasham asked why this was being done and was told, 'Everything is going to change, you're going to have to make a choice between your mum and me'. He had also piled up six bin liners, full of papers, in the hall, and placed a large maroon suitcase in the lounge. The entire family, apart from one child, then went to the takeaway where they had a family conference, Rahman again accusing his wife of having an affair. Rezia then left at around 9pm, with the children.

Rahman later phoned home to ask if the phone had been disconnected, something he had asked for because of the alleged large bill. When told it had not been disconnected he instructed that the line was cut, and this was carried out. The shop was again closed early, at midnight, when Rahman and his sons returned home.

However, at 3am the following morning, Rahman called at the home of Stanley Baker, a casual employee, with two full carrier bags and a suitcase, brought in from his van. He asked Stanley to look after them as he was 'not very well. I am leaving Southampton, I have just had a gutful of the family'. He also asked if he could stay there, but was told that Stanley was not allowed lodgers.

At midday that day, Thursday 20 January, Kasham, their son, saw his parents leave for the Takeaway in the van.

A representative of Yellow Pages, Harriet Batchelor, had made an appointment to see Rahman at the takeaway between 3pm and 3.30pm that day, but when she arrived at 3.20pm the van was not parked outside, as was normal, the shop was in darkness and the door and grilles were locked. She rattled the grilles and letter box and remained until around 3.30pm before leaving.

At 6pm that evening Paul Brown, a refrigeration engineer, called, by appointment, at the takeaway to check on some fridges which were not working correctly. He also found the premises secure and in darkness.

Earlier, at around 4pm, their son Abul returned to the family home in Burgess Road and found that his brother and sisters were alone, with no sign of their mother. This was very unusual. He therefore went to the takeaway, finding it locked, in darkness and no sign of his father's van. He returned home and by 9.15pm all the children were at home without their parents.

The children phoned friends and relatives, but none of them had seen the couple that day. The eldest sons, Kamal and Abul, then visited Stanley Baker and were told about Rahman collecting his suitcase and carrier bags. By 11pm, when nothing had still been heard from their parents, the police were contacted and told their parents were missing.

Officers attended and took details, but as there were no spare keys to the takeaway they could only circulate details of the family's van.

At 1pm the following day, Friday 21 January, officers again called at the takeaway premises, but as all efforts to find duplicate keys had failed, decided this time to force an entry. The two padlocks securing the grille were removed using bolt croppers and the heavy wooden door forced using an approved 'enforcer'.

On entering and searching they found Rezia's body, dressed in traditional clothing, lying in the cellar, close to the bottom of the stairs. There was a large amount of blood surrounding her body and on a chest freezer directly behind her head. The lower half of her body and head was covered by two white work coats, and on lifting them it was clear that she was dead with massive and extensive head injuries. The scene was sealed off and Alex Dodd, scenes of crime officer, attended with senior police photographer Barry Hill. Photographs were taken of the scene, including fingerprints and bare footprint marks made in blood.

A post-mortem was carried out at 6.50pm that day by Dr Anscombe, who found Rezia had sustained extensive fracturing of her skull and face, with a severe degree of mutilation to the face as a result of what he estimated to be between three and four

Khalilur Rahman. (*Hampshire Constabulary History Society*)

dozen blows to the head and face with a moderately heavy and blunt instrument. Her face was so badly battered as to be unrecognisable.

A murder investigation was undertaken, led by Det.Insp. Chris Seymour, with the codename Operation Markham and Khalilur Rahman was circulated as wanted for questioning, with his photograph given to the press and published on Saturday 22 January.

At 3.30pm that day Rahman called on a friend, Abdul Jalil, at his home in Swaton Road, Poplar, London. He appeared depressed and when Abdul said he had been told that Rezia had been killed, Rahman replied, 'Maybe her boyfriend killed her and he is trying to blame me.' He left the house at 4pm, saying he was going to return to Southampton to see his children.

At around 5.50pm the same day Rahman went into an East Enders mini-market in Bow Road, London, in a hysterical state, saying he had been mugged. The shopkeeper phoned the police but Rahman left before they arrived.

About 10 minutes later Rahman approached two ladies walking along Bow Road and asked them to call the police. He said that some people were trying to kill him and take his money. The ladies used the police telephone box outside Bow Street police station and PC Potter arrived shortly afterwards.

Rahman told him he had been chased out of his friend's house in Swaton Road by his enemies, who had guns and knives. Rahman was taken to Limehouse police station while the officer had a check made at the house in Swaton Road.

When PC Potter returned from Swaton Road and told Rahman that the incident had not occurred, Rahman said, 'Well, you should have heard of me as I have been charged with murder at Southampton'. PC Potter then made enquiries with Southampton police and as a result arrested Rahman on suspicion of murdering his wife. After caution Rahman replied, 'I don't care, I just want to see my children.' While he was detained at Limehouse police station a forensic team attended, taking possession of his clothing, various body samples, including taking inked impressions of his bare feet.

He was then taken to Southampton Central police station and interviewed by DC Jason Attwell and DC Skerry. He gave an account of leaving his home in Burgess Road at midday on Thursday 20 January, taking a bag with passports and cash as he intended going to London to make arrangements for his family to travel to Mecca. He said his wife was aware of this. He went to the takeaway with his wife, which she left at around

2pm, and 10 minutes later he also left, locking the premises, putting up the grilles and padlocking them.

He said he then drove his van to London, but got lost, and then gave a rambling account of being taken against his will by different people to various London addresses, all of which were checked and found to have no knowledge of Rahman having been there. He stated that the men had taken his keys and personal property, including his mobile phone, and told him they had killed his wife and were going to kill him. He said he managed to escape from the house and ran to Bow Road, where he first went into a card shop and asked them to call the police, then left and ran down the road until he saw two ladies who called the police for him.

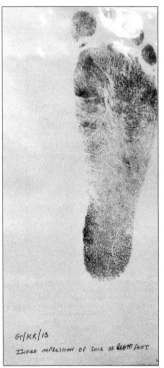

GT/KR/13

INKED IMPRESSION of SOLE of RIGHT FOOT

Rahman's right foot impression. (*Hampshire Constabulary History Society*)

He denied ever having assaulted his wife; denied thinking she was having an affair and said he had not seen his wife since she left the Takeaway on Thursday. He strongly denied having killed her and having any explanation as to why she should be killed. He insisted he had been in London at the time of her death and that it had probably been carried out by one of his business enemies.

A forensic examination of his jacket revealed a very small spot of blood, later confirmed as his wife's and a fingerprint found in the basement, containing a fragment of her blood, was found to be Rahman's. An inked impression of Rahman's right foot was also found to be identical to those found near the body.

Stanley Baker, when interviewed, stated that Rahman had said to him, when in the takeaway around the time of the murder, 'If the police ask any questions, my wife is trying to kill me.' When asked what he meant Rahman had replied, 'I think she is trying to poison me'.

At 10.52pm on Monday 24 January he was charged with his wife's murder, cautioned, and he replied, 'I didn't do it'. Begum appeared before Mr Justice Patrick Elias at Winchester Crown Court on Wednesday 15 November 2000 and in the course of a three-week trial continued to insist that his wife had died at the hands of either one of his business enemies, a stranger or her supposed lover. He claimed he had gone to London to get tickets for a family pilgrimage to Mecca.

The jurors were unable to reach a verdict after five and a half hours deliberation and the trial was adjourned to the following day, Friday 1 December, when, after a total of nine hours deliberation, the jury returned a unanimous guilty verdict of murder.

It was then revealed that Rahman, who had shown not a scrap of remorse following his arrest and during his trial, had a previous conviction for grievous bodily harm. He was told by Mr Justice Elias, 'It is a terrible thing you have done. You brought great tragedy on your family, bringing them great misery and distress.' He then sentenced Rahman to life imprisonment.

The unfortunate Rezia Begum is buried in unmarked grave D8-220 in Hollybrook Cemetery.

2000 – RICHARD HUGHES – BLED TO DEATH

Top: Richard Hughes' home in Millbrook Road West.

left: Richard Hughes. (*Hampshire Constabulary History Society*)

Bachelor Richard William Myles Hughes, 29, a computer enthusiast, lived in a ground floor flat in Millbrook Road West, a community-type housing block where the majority of the residents had, or were recovering from, differing personal problems.

Richard, who was well spoken, 6ft 3in tall and of heavy build, was regarded by his friends as a 'gentle giant' and affectionately known as 'Big Un'. He had lived in the flat for two years and was said to have had drink and drug problems. Although unemployed, he was in receipt of some income from a trust fund set up by his late father and was known to be generous and quick to buy a round of drinks for his friends.

On Friday 24 November 2000 other residents became concerned as he had not been seen for several days, and repeated knocking on his

Freemantle Baptist Church, Testwood Road.

flat door had no response. The police were called, made normal routine enquiries but then decided to force open the door late that evening. Richard's bloodstained body was found lying there, its condition suggested he had died several days earlier. There were signs of severe head injuries but no indication as to how he had come by them. A murder squad was formed, under Det.Ch.Insp. Paul Clark, with the codename Operation Barnfield, and his photograph circulated in the local press with an appeal for information.

As a result of the media appeal, Roy Hendy, pastor of Millbrook Baptist Church in Testwood Road, contacted the police to tell them that on Sunday 19 November 2000, he had arrived at his church to find members of his congregation helping Richard, who had blood pouring from his face. He was sitting on a church seat with a towel wrapped around his face to reduce the flow. He refused to be taken to hospital, as he had a phobia about it, but agreed to be taken to his home nearby.

Pastor Hendy therefore drove him to his flat and sat with him for about 10 minutes while Richard went to his bathroom and cleaned himself up. The pastor left his business card with Richard and returned later that night, and again the following day, to see how he was, but there was no reply. Mr Hendy told the police that he did not think that Richard's injuries were life-threatening, otherwise he would not have left him in the first instance.

Further information came from Wendy Allen, the landlady of the Park Hotel in Shirley. She said that when Richard's photograph was shown in the *Echo* she recognised him as one of her regulars. Her customers were talking about it, saying there had been a suggestion that he might have been interested in little children. One of her customers, Paul Stanton, 22, of Varna Road, Freemantle, told her he had given Richard 'a slapping' after seeing him with his hand on the bottom of a two and a half-year-old girl.

Karaoke pub entertainer Michael Jones also mentioned that Stanton had told him he had kicked Richard and that his friend, Justin Byles, 26, of Irving Road, Maybush, had 'gone over the top' by hitting him with a bottle.

Charmaine Page, a family friend of James Robinson, 20, of Darwin Road, Shirley, was told by him that he had been involved in the attack but had only hit Richard three times. He also said that Justin Byles had 'gone over the top' and kept hitting him with a bottle, carrying on hitting even after the bottle had broken.

As a result of extensive police enquiries all three men were detained for questioning. A story emerged that Richard had been initially punched by Robinson when they left the Maybush public house the previous Saturday night.

He was then forcibly taken by the other two to a nearby cutway where Stanton struck him in the ribs. Byles then struck Richard with a Budweiser beer bottle, hitting him until the glass smashed and then continued to strike with the broken bottle. The attack came about because the men believed he had indecently assaulted a young girl.

When they left him they ordered him to leave Southampton and, in fact, visited his flat the following day to ensure he had left, but had no reply.

It therefore appeared that Richard had somehow managed to stagger home from the Maybush public house and gone to the Baptist Church the following morning, from where he was taken home by the pastor. Because of refusing hospital treatment he had then bled to death.

The Maybush public house, the scene of the attack. (*Dave Goddard*) It is now derelict, with the site awaiting development.

All three were charged with murder and appeared before Mr Justice Toulson at Winchester Crown Court on 4 July 2001, where they pleaded not guilty to charges of murder and manslaughter. After the witnesses Pastor Hendy, Wendy Allen, Michael Jones and Charmaine Page had given evidence, forensic odontologist David Lewin, one of the country's leading experts, was called.

He stated that 10 separate injuries on Richard's face coincided perfectly with a gold ring worn by James Robinson. He said, 'These marks are consistent with the size, shape and pattern of the ring. In my opinion the top of the ring fits the marks. The degree of force indicated by the marks is not a friendly pat. It would require considerable force. It is not pleasant.'

On the eighth day of the trial there were lengthy legal arguments about the charge of murder. To sustain a charge of murder it must be proved that the offender intended to kill or was reckless as to the likely consequence of their action, so their state of mind at the time of the killing is a crucial factor. Manslaughter can be established when the fact of killing is not in dispute, rather the motive behind it.

The end result was that all three pleaded guilty to manslaughter, accepting that each had played a part in an unlawful killing. They were remanded in custody to await pre-sentence reports, and when they reappeared on Friday 27 July 2001 the judge said, 'Mr Hughes died as a result of an assault which was cowardly, unprovoked, sustained and vicious. The supposed indecent assault did not begin to excuse the violent way you reacted.'

Paul Stanton and Justin Byles were each sentenced to five years imprisonment and James Robinson to four years in a young offenders' institution.

2001 – DEVON ADAMSON – A CRIME OF PASSION

Devon Anthony Adamson, 22, attended Catholic schools in his native Kingston, Jamaica before he trained as a welder and obtained work there. He lived with his mother, who said he was 'a loving son', but also sometimes stayed with his girlfriend. He had a four-year-old son from a previous relationship and was due to become a father again. In July 2001 he decided to come to England to seek work and also visit friends.

He settled in Southampton, where he shared lodgings in Oxford Avenue with Keiona Brissett, 21, a fellow Jamaican. Brissett was an illegal immigrant who had arrived in Southampton the previous May.

The Oxford Avenue lodgings.

The Queensland Tavern (now turned into residential apartments). (*Dave Goddard*)

The two men were regular drinkers at the nearby Queensland Tavern, often playing pool together, but their initial friendship ceased when they had a disagreement over a 16-year-old girl living in the house. This culminated in a bitter argument inside the Queensland on the afternoon of Monday 2 September 2001, so fierce that both men were thrown out.

They continued to fight outside, in Exmoor Road, where Devon punched Brissett extremely hard, with the sovereign rings on his fingers acting as a knuckleduster. Brissett staggered back to his lodgings in Oxford Avenue to recover, but then realised that he had left his mobile phone in the public house. He returned to collect it, but armed himself with a kitchen knife, taking it, as he later said, 'to protect myself'. He met Devon in the street outside the public house just before 5pm and a second argument broke out.

The men came to blows again, but this time Brissett pushed the kitchen knife, which had a blade over six inches long, with a single thrust into the left side of Devon's chest. He then ran off when he saw Devon was bleeding heavily from his chest.

Devon, in a semi-collapsed state, staggered along Exmoor Road towards the nearby Royal South Hants Hospital in Graham Road, supported by a passing fellow Jamaican. They managed to enter the main corridor, next to the blood clinic, where he collapsed. Although this hospital has no accident & emergency facilities, two nurses were quickly on the scene, having been called by a porter, and were joined by a doctor from the blood clinic.

They called an ambulance and the paramedics placed a pad on his chest to try to stop the bleeding but their continued efforts were in vain and he was pronounced dead at the scene. The police attended within minutes and Exmoor Road was sealed off while a murder investigation, with the code name Operation Georgian, got under way, under the command of Det.Supt Mike Lane. A subsequent post-mortem confirmed that death was due to a single stab wound to the heart.

There was no immediate evidence available showing the involvement of Keiona Brissett so over the ensuing three weeks extensive police activity was carried out by the 50-strong murder squad to identify the attacker. As a result of differing information received from the resident immigrant community, a series of police raids were carried out on premises in Oxford Avenue, Northumberland Road, Lodge Road, and Addison Road in Sarisbury Green.

Exmoor Road, from the Queensland Tavern, looking towards the Royal South Hants Hospital.

A week after the murder an eight-hour operation was carried out across the Newtown and Nicholstown areas, when 600 motorists and 400 pedestrians were stopped and questioned. Posters, in English as well as two Asian and Indian dialects, were distributed around the inner city area in the hope of encouraging witnesses to come forward. They included details of the silver and black Nike Max Air trainers worn by Devon. He had entered the hospital barefooted and his trainers were found in the street near the Queensland Tavern.

The enquiries came to an end when Keiona Brissett surrendered to the police at Gatwick Airport, where he had intended boarding a flight to Orlando. He had told the airport reception staff, 'I am tired of running, I never wanted to be a criminal' and readily admitted the stabbing. He was transferred to Southampton, charged with the murder and appeared before Mr Justice Butterfield at Winchester Crown Court on Monday 3 September 2002.

He pleaded 'not guilty' to murder but 'guilty' to manslaughter. This was accepted by the prosecution and he was sentenced to five years imprisonment. On his release in February 2005 Brissett was deported to Jamaica.

Devon Adamson is buried in Hollybrook Cemetery, in unmarked plot L21-152

Keiona Brissett. (*Hampshire Constabulary History Society*)

2001 – ANDREW HEATH – A SINGLE PUNCH AT LEISURE WORLD

Twenty-eight-year-old bachelor Andrew Michael Heath, of Viking Close, Lordshill, had too much to drink when he left the Leisure World complex around 4.35pm on Sunday 21 January 2001. He was, in fact, treble the drink-drive limit as he mingled with the several hundred individuals leaving the premises. This no doubt explains his behaviour outside the building in a queue for a taxi, when he became very annoyed and frustrated as a couple tried to take the taxi he thought should have been his.

He lashed out in temper, attempting to strike 19-year-old Oliver, a carpenter from Meridith Towers, Tunstall Road, Thornhill. However, his inebriated condition meant that he missed completely, hitting, instead, Oliver's girlfriend, Kassidy Strasser, leaving her in tears.

Leisure World doormen were present and prevented several of the crowd from retaliating against Heath, but after a few minutes Oliver managed to get to Heath and landed a heavy blow on his face, knocking him to the ground.

Heath fell so heavily that his head struck the pavement with a sickening thud, heard by all those around him, and he immediately became unconscious. Oliver nudged the prone Heath a couple of times and when he realised the extent of the injury, ran away with his girlfriend. Unfortunately for him, in his panic he dropped his passport in West Quay Road as he did so. They ran to the nearby coach station in Western Esplanade where they persuaded two men to share a taxi back to Thornhill.

Meanwhile, the police and ambulance had been called and Andrew Heath was taken to

The overall scene of the attack outside Leisure World. (*Hampshire Constabulary History Society*)

the General Hospital and detained. The police were soon told about the dropped passport, enabling them to arrest Oliver at his flat in the early hours of the morning. When arrested he said, 'He went to hit me, missed me and hit my girlfriend'.

When first interviewed by Det.Con. Neil Cutting at Central Police Station he said, 'A lot of people knew Kassidy had been hit and they were all trying to hit him, but nothing happened because the bouncers were there. Suddenly he came back from nowhere. We struck each other and he fell to the floor. I ran scared.'

Andrew Heath, who had suffered a fractured skull, never regained consciousness and died two days later. The police investigation, under the code name Operation Vicarage, then became a murder enquiry.

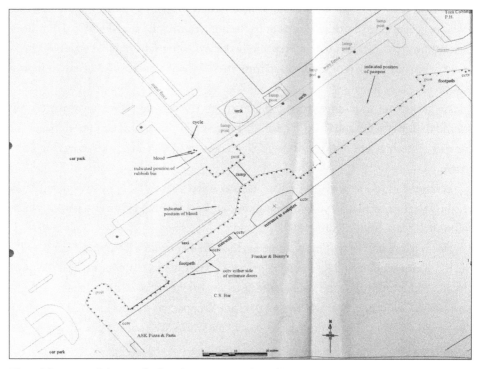

Plan of the scene of the attack, showing areas mentioned in witness statements. (*Hampshire Constabulary History Society*)

Bloodstains on the pavement where Andrew Heath fell. (*Hampshire Constabulary History Society*)

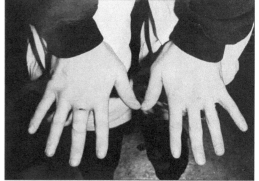

Police photograph of Oliver's hands, showing abrasions. (*Hampshire Constabulary History Society*)

Oliver was charged with the murder and appeared before Mr Justice Silber at Winchester Crown Court on 16 November 2001, when he pleaded 'not guilty'. This was accepted by the prosecution and the case proceeded on the alternative charge of manslaughter, to which he also pleaded 'not guilty'.

During the week-long trial Oliver insisted he acted in self-defence. He sobbed when he gave evidence, saying, 'It is just tragic, I didn't mean anyone to die.' He said he had only struck Heath because he was walking towards him with clenched fists, looking aggressive. He added that he was frightened because 'he was big and he looked like he was going to hurt me. It was just one blow, a jab. It hit his cheek and he fell over. I wasn't expecting that to happen. He went straight down.'

When the judge summed up at the conclusion of the evidence, he told the jury, 'You must focus on the punch to see if he, Oliver, was acting in self-defence when he threw it. Did Oliver honestly believe it was necessary to defend himself when he threw the fatal punch. Your task is to decide whether the use of that punch was reasonable.'

After deliberating for four hours, the jury of nine women and three men failed to agree a verdict and were sent home for the night. The following day, after deliberating for a further three hours, they returned a verdict of guilty of manslaughter.

The judge then told Oliver, 'One of the reasons for this tragedy is that your victim, Mr Heath, had been drinking heavily. This meant he was unlikely or unable to use protective reflexes by putting his hands out and he therefore suffered the fatal injury. I regard your attack as being one of revenge and retaliation. The courts make it very clear that violence of the streets is to be punished. I accept that this was an unfortunate accident but it was an act of revenge. There was a gap of about three minutes after the attack on your girlfriend but you still went to deliver this blow of moderate to severe force.'

He then adjourned the case for a probation report, and on his return, on 22 November, sentenced Oliver to nine months imprisonment.

Because of the time he had spent in custody on remand, it meant that, in fact, Oliver only had another five weeks to spend in youth custody.

2001 – EDWARD MADDICK – DUMPED UNDER A HEDGE

Six-foot Edward Stanley Maddick, 45, of Bampton Close, Millbrook, had battled against debilitating myoclonic epilepsy for over five years and was registered disabled. A builder by trade, and a workaholic by nature, his condition had stopped him working in 1997. He walked with a distinctive gait, as he had poor co-ordination and could not walk far without having to stop to get his balance. He also had a problem with his speech. Edward was often

Edward Maddick. (*Hampshire Constabulary History Society*)

unable to wash and dress himself without the help of his wife Caroline, 44, a Special Needs Assistant, his partner of 26 years. But in spite of these disabilities he remained cheerful and contented with a close-knit large extended family across Southampton, including his daughter Kelly and son Warren living at home.

On Saturday 28 July 2001 Edward spent the evening enjoying a few drinks in pubs around the Shirley area, as he did about once a month. He wasn't a heavy drinker but enjoyed this regular outing. At about 11pm he entered the Tramways public house in Shirley High Street and left the premises just before 1.10am, after sharing some time with friends.

Tramways as it was in 2001 – it has now resumed its former name of Crown Hotel. (*Dave Goddard*)

He slowly made his way home along a cutway leading from Tebourba Way towards William Macleod Way and the Tesco supermarket adjoining Tebourba Way, as was his normal custom. What happened there will never be fully known. What is known, however, is that he was seen between 1.30am and 1.55am that Sunday morning lying on grass adjacent to the pathway, apparently asleep. That was consistent with his illness; he may have needed a rest. The cutway was well lit and frequently used by residents, so he would have help if he needed it.

At just after that time young Serena Parker and her boyfriend saw a man lying on the path, next to a drain, and assumed he was a drunk, probably a tramp, who was sleeping it off. It is virtually certain that he was Edward, recovering after possibly falling down or having a seizure.

At around 2.40am he was again seen by a man on the opposite side of the footpath, pushed up hard against a fence. He was lying on his stomach, groaning and appeared to be trying to move. The witness believed he was drunk so carried on walking. He was found nearly eight hours later, at around 9am, by a dog walker, but this time clearly dead, with serious head injuries. His bloody and battered body, with appalling injuries, was under a hedge in the pathway.

The police were called and a 300strong murder squad, with the code name Operation Erskine, was rapidly formed under the leadership of Det.Supt John James. The initial examination at the scene revealed Edward's empty wallet and some loose change on the pathway near his body. It was therefore suspected that he had been the victim of a 'mugging'.

Top: The entrance to the cutway, from Tebourba Way.

Bottom: The cutway, showing the drain and the hedge opposite, where the body was found.

A subsequent post-mortem by a Home Office pathologist revealed that Edward Maddick had suffered a fractured skull, nose, jaw, cheekbone and ribs. The injuries were consistent with him having been repeatedly kicked and possibly also stamped on. A bloodstained mark on his shirt, after forensic tests, established that the killer had been wearing Adidas trainers.

His wife later told the police that her husband often walked that route as it was off the main road and quieter. The drain where he was found was one which he would sit on for a rest if he became tired.

Detectives examined the CCTV camera footage and saw that several people had used the footpath between 1.30am and 3am that morning and made a media appeal, showing Edward's photograph, for them to come forward. One incident was of special interest, a man filmed running out of the cutway and across Tebourba Way.

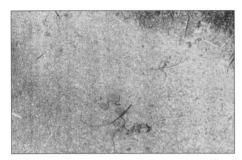

Left: Loose coins and (right) the empty wallet found near the body. (*Hampshire Constabulary History Society*)

Aerial view of the scene, the white arrow showing where Maddick was found. (*Hampshire Constabulary History Society*)

Enquiries then centred on an incident that had taken place at around 3.30am that Sunday morning at the 24-hour Alldays convenience store in Shirley Road. Sgt Mark Harper of Shirley police had attended as a result of Barry Whittle, 20, of Hill Lane, having been involved in an unprovoked fight with two men. The sergeant saw Whittle, who appeared aggressive and very agitated, pacing around with clenched fists and walking up to an advertising board as if to punch it. He was clearly under the influence, his clothing was bloodstained and he had sustained some injuries but declined medical treatment. No action was needed and he left the scene to go home.

Further enquiries showed that he had been arrested the previous night for kicking a man in the head during an argument with two strangers in Ocean Village, outside a convenience store. The victim, Peter Wallace, was initially thought to have life-threatening injuries, but recovered. Whittle, 6ft 2in and from Northern Ireland, was therefore on police bail for this assault.

He was re-arrested and when questioned about the attack on Mr Maddick, he admitted having used the cutway at the material time. He said he had left a party in William Macleod Way and the cutway was the natural route to take in order to arrive at the Dell Guest House in Hill Lane, where he was a resident. He stated that while walking through the pathway he had been attacked by a 20-year-old man but they had merely exchanged punches. He insisted that the man could not have been 45-year-old Edward Maddick as the man he punched was definitely only in his 20s.

He was detained for further enquiries, and when the police visited his guest house in Hill Lane they interviewed a 15-year-old schoolgirl who also lived in the building. She said that Whittle had burst into her room at the guest house around 4am and explained that his trainers, T-shirt and jogging bottoms were stained with blood following a fight in Shirley.

A man had offered him some money but he said he didn't want his money and then blacked out. When he woke up he was 'stamping on the bloke's head'. The girl added that Whittle demonstrated by jumping up and down at the end of the bed and she saw his trainers were bloodstained. He took them off and asked her to put them under her brother's bed, but then took them back and left the room.

Whittle was interviewed about this and asked for the whereabouts of the bloodstained trainers and clothing. He said he had thrown them into the back of a dustcart on the Monday morning. This was confirmed when the refuse collector was traced and said he had seen a young man run from the back of the property in Hill Lane and throw a white plastic bag into the back of the truck. Whittle refused to make any comment in reply to further questions put to him.

Det.Supt James planned a search to recover the trainers and clothing, believing it would only take a few days to locate them in the landfill site. This would be compelling

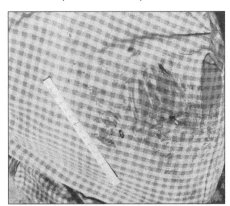

Bloodstained mark on Edward Maddick's shirt and the soles of Adidas trainers. (*Hampshire Constabulary History Society*)

forensic evidence. However, he then discovered that, in fact, it would involve around 1,000 tons of material that had already been treated with chemicals and it would take 16 people eight weeks to complete the search, at a cost of £150,000. The decision was then taken to call off the search both on the grounds of cost and because it would have resulted in 'an unacceptable abstraction of frontline staff'.

SoC officers searching refuse and a small part of the pile yet to be searched. (*Hampshire Constabulary History Society***)**

During the evening of Friday 3 August an identification parade was held at Southsea police station where Whittle was positively identified as (a) the man at the Dell Guest House making significant admissions to the assault and disposing of his bloodstained trainers, (b) having attended the party at William Macleod Way and leaving in the early hours of the morning and (c) the man involved in the fracas at Alldays shop at 3.30am 29 July seen wearing bloodstained footwear.

Whittle was formally charged with the murder at 11am Saturday 4 August 2001 and appeared before Mr Justice William Taylor at Winchester Crown Court on 16 May 2002, when he pleaded 'not guilty'. By then the unfortunate Edward Maddick had been cremated.

A crucial witness was Whittle's neighbour, Dyan Thomas. After Whittle heard about the murder over the radio later that day he had entered her room, very upset, with his hands on his head, saying, 'Oh my God, I think I murdered that man'. He then made several phone calls, in her presence, to his stepfather in Northern Ireland and told him he had murdered a man and did not know what to do.

He was crying and said his stepfather had told him to hand himself in. Miss Thomas left with Whittle, at 9.30am on Tuesday 31 July, to visit Shirley police station.

En route, and before deciding not to hand himself in, he told her that a fight had taken place on the footpath in Tebourba Way and it was an accident. She told the court, 'Barry said he punched him and he fell down, got back up and said to Barry to take his money. Barry punched him again, he fell to the ground and the man threw his money at him. Barry said he then blacked out and when he came round he was jumping up and down on the man's head. He then dragged him by the ankles and rolled him into a hedge. He said he thought the man was unconscious and did not realise he had killed him. When he was saying this he was hysterical.'

At one stage in the trial the jury, together with counsels for prosecution and defence, the officers in the case, and court staff, but not Whittle, were taken to the footpath in Tebourba Way to see the scene for themselves. Armed with sketch plans, photographs, pen and paper, the eight men and four women, walked around the area.

Whittle also gave evidence, insisting the man he fought with was only in his 20s, said he had taken a small amount of ecstasy, smoked cannabis, snorted a small amount of cocaine and had drunk some Guinness and Southern Comfort on the night Edward Maddick was attacked.

On Tuesday 28 May after deliberating for under four hours, the jury returned a unanimous verdict of 'not guilty' to both murder and manslaughter and Whittle collapsed in the dock. There were angry scenes in the court, whereby Judge Taylor adjourned proceedings for around 10 minutes, but Whittle, on being discharged, left the dock grinning broadly.

This was dispelled shortly after his acquittal when he was sentenced to two years imprisonment for the attack on a man at Ocean Village the night before the murder. However, because of the time spent on remand he only spent a further week in prison.

There is, however, a twist in the tale, taken from accounts fully reported in the national press.

He again stood trial in August 2002, this time at Bournemouth Crown Court, charged with attacking a woman in April 2001 by holding a knife to her throat, hitting

her legs with an iron bar and threatening to set fire to her home. He was cleared of all charges at the end of a three-day trial.

In May 2003 he was charged with carrying out an armed robbery at a Londonderry insurance company but this was dropped after a co-defendant pleaded guilty.

In 2005 he was sentenced to three years imprisonment at Laganside Crown Court, Belfast, after deliberately driving a car at two brothers and seriously injuring them. The original charges of attempted murder were dropped

Barry Whittle. (*Hampshire Constabulary History Society*)

after he pleaded guilty to lesser charges of dangerous driving and grievous bodily harm.

In July 2008, six years after being acquitted of the murder of Edward Maddick, he walked into Londonderry Strand Road police station and confessed to the murder, saying he 'couldn't live with it'.

However, although the Crown Prosecution Service asked the Court of Appeal for a fresh trial, the Lord Chief Justice, Lord Igor Judge, dismissed the request, saying the admission did not amount to compelling evidence of Whittle's guilt.

The police have officially stated that the case is now closed.

2001 – AUDREY TARRANT – A SAD OUTCOME

Audrey Ann Tarrant, 45, was an alcoholic who had seriously fallen out with her husband. Lee, 21, was unhappy about the disagreement and on the evening of Saturday 8 September 2001 invited them to his apartment in Lydgate Road, Thornhill, for a reconciliatory meal.

Some drinking took place during the evening, resulting in a drunken argument, in the course of which Lee lost his temper and struck Audrey a heavy blow behind her right ear. There did not appear to be any serious injury, no more than a reddening of the skin, but two days later she became unwell and was admitted to the Southampton General Hospital.

The Lydgate Road apartment block.

It was suspected she had sustained a blood clot but she refused the possibility of surgery and discharged herself two days later, returning to her home in Sycamore Road, Shirley Warren.

However, she again became unwell, this time more seriously, and was re-admitted to the neurological ward high care unit where, in spite of all their efforts, she died at 8.15am on Saturday 22 September.

A post-mortem revealed she had died as a result of the blow behind her ear and Lee was arrested the following Friday and charged with her murder. He was remanded in custody and appeared before Judge Michael Brodrick at the Hampshire Crown Court at Winchester on 2 October 2002.

He pleaded 'not guilty' to murder but 'guilty' to manslaughter. Lee wrote a letter to the judge, in which he said, 'A day does not pass when I do not deeply regret my actions and the hurt and pain I have caused. My guilt will stay with me for the rest of my life.'

The judge said that Lee had already served the equivalent of a two-year jail sentence while on remand and was not considered a risk to the public.

He added, 'Sentence in a case like this is extremely difficult because the family of the deceased, the media and the public will focus almost exclusively on the fact that a wife

and mother has died. I believe other considerations have to be taken into account. You did not intend to kill or cause really serious bodily harm.'

He then sentenced Lee to a two-year community rehabilitation order and he was able to walk free from the court.

Audrey Tarrant was cremated but her ashes are buried in her maiden name, Aldworth family plot M17-147, in Hollybrook Cemetery.

Her grave is marked with a plain wooden cross simply marked 'Wife' and 'Mum'.

2002 – ANTHONY GUNN – DEATH OF A POPULAR MAN

Anthony Gunn, 37, a scaffolder living in Outer Circle, Coxford, had moved to Southampton from his native Cumbria in 2000 and obtained work at Fawley Oil Refinery. Father of a son and two daughters, by 2002 he was looking forward to marrying his partner, Clare Stewart, 30, in May that year. He was a very popular man, described by his fiancée as 'always happy-go-lucky and fantastic'.

Clare Stewart's world came to an end just before midnight on Sunday 8 December, 2002. Two groups, each inflamed by drink, had passed through each other while walking in opposite directions along Park Road, when some insults passed between them. It was quickly followed by an exchange of blows that rapidly developed into a large-scale disturbance. The groups, still fighting, then moved to Mansion Road, at the junction with Queenstown Road.

One group, who had been drinking in the Star & Garter, included Anthony Gunn and the other, who had been drinking in the Shirley Social Club, contained unemployed Richard Smith, 22, of nearby Victory Crescent, Freemantle. Smith was walking home with his girlfriend, Charlene Dawson, 18, who said she had been hit by someone in Anthony Gunn's group. This had sparked off the fighting, but Anthony tried to break up the two groups and calm the situation.

Mansion Road, the scene of the stabbing.

Unfortunately for Anthony, Richard Smith, upset by the alleged assault on his girlfriend, left the fighting and ran to the adjacent Queenstown Road flat of his friend, William Turlin, 21, who was watching TV. Smith shouted through the letterbox, 'Help, let me in, my girlfriend's getting beaten up'. He was let into the premises by Turlin and went into the kitchen. He grabbed an eight inch kitchen knife and, followed by Turlin, returned to the scene shouting, 'I will do you up like a kebab. I will carve you like a kebab' while brandishing the knife. Someone, with a northern voice, almost certainly Anthony Gunn, said, 'Don't be stupid, put the knife down' in an effort to calm Smith.

A few seconds later several of the crowd saw Smith stab Anthony several times in the stomach and he fell to the pavement in a collapsed condition. Most of the crowd then rapidly dispersed, with both Smith and Turlin running to Turlin's flat. Once there Turlin took the knife from Smith and cleaned it in the kitchen sink, to destroy any possible evidence.

The police and ambulance were called and soon discovered that Anthony had been stabbed in the stomach and was in a critical condition. Their immediate enquiries were hampered by most of those remaining being drunk and the poor light conditions for the neighbours looking out of their windows during the course of the fighting.

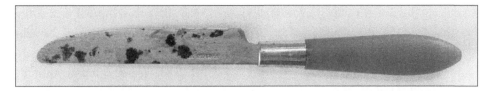

The knife recovered from William Turlin's flat. (*Hampshire Constabulary History Society*)

Some of those remaining, however, were able to point out Turlin's flat, where the two men had fled, and the occupants, Turlin and Martin Gelder, were detained. Smith and his girlfriend had left the scene before the police arrived. The flat was searched and a knife was recovered.

Smith was traced and arrested late in the evening of Monday 9 December and taken to Bitterne police station. Blood was found on Smith's trainers, which were seized for forensic examination.

Anthony was taken to the General Hospital where emergency surgery was performed on two stab wounds in his back and in a lung. The situation changed dramatically when Anthony Gunn, in spite of intensive medical care, died at 5pm the following Tuesday 10 December.

The initial grievous bodily harm investigation was now a murder one, given the codename Operation Eastpark, headed by Det.Insp. Alison Scott and Det.Sgt Stephen Edbury.

A subsequent post-mortem revealed that Anthony had received three knife thrusts, one of which had penetrated his back to the full length of the blade, puncturing his lung.

All three men were questioned, in the course of which Turlin admitted having cleaned the knife taken by Smith, but denied taking part in the fighting. Smith refused to admit using the knife or taking part in the fighting by answering 'no comment' to questions. A warrant was granted to allow a further 36 hours of detention, but although no admissions were made he was charged on 12 December with the murder of Anthony Gunn.

The blood on Smith's trainers was found to have Anthony Gunn's DNA and he was accordingly charged with the murder and Turlin with assisting him. Both appeared before Judge Michael Broderick at Winchester Crown Court in August 2003 and pleaded not guilty.

Prior to the hearing Anthony Gunn's funeral had taken place in his home town of Cleator Moor, Cumbria, his popularity shown by over 1,000 mourners attending the packed ceremony. There was no doubt that he was hugely popular and the funeral was described as the biggest the town had ever seen.

During the course of the murder trial Richard Smith described himself as 'a skinny wimp with learning difficulties' and told the jury that he had run away from the fight. He said he came from a broken home and had moved to Southampton when he was 16, indulging in petty crime but with no record of violence. He denied stabbing Anthony.

The landlord of the Star & Garter public house in Waterloo Road, Freemantle, gave evidence that Anthony had been drinking there on the night of the attack. He added, 'I have never seen him angry. He was a gentle giant. I have seen him drunk on many occasions but I have never seen him lose his temper or offer violence to anyone, whether drunk or sober.'

At the conclusion of the three-week trial the jury cleared William Turlin of the charge of assisting an offender, and he was freed. He later said, 'My thoughts are with Tony Gunn's family, who are all lovely people. I would like to say to them that I'm sorry I was put in this position and was unnecessarily involved in this matter. I would also like to pass my condolences to Smith's family. I have got to live with what I have witnessed for the rest of my life.'

Smith, however, was found guilty of the murder and the judge said, 'The grief that has been caused to Anthony Gunn's family and friends must be very difficult for any of us in court to imagine.' He then sentenced Smith to life imprisonment.

The court was also told that while Smith was in custody on remand he had tried to break out of his cell. Bricks had been removed from a wall, almost enough to get his head through, and he was found in possession of a home-made rope and grappling hook. For this he received a two-year concurrent sentence.

There was a sequel four years later when Smith appealed against the length of his sentence.

After reviewing the case at London's Royal Court of Justice, Mr Justice Pitchford ruled that he must serve a minimum tariff of 15 years. Even taking time spent on remand into account it meant that Smith cannot apply for parole until early 2018. The court heard that Smith has previous convictions for dishonesty, including burglary, assaulting the police in 2000, having a bladed article in public and attempting to escape lawful custody.

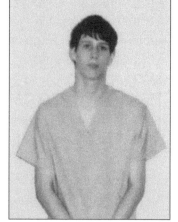

Richard Smith. (*Hampshire Constabulary History Society*)

2002 – IAN DAVID O'BRIEN – 'SOLVING A JIGSAW PUZZLE'

A murder investigation, under the codename 'Operation Shaftsbury', started just after 11pm on the evening of Wednesday 6 February 2002. The fully clothed body of a man with severe head injuries had been found earlier by church leader Paul O'Neill and his friend in a private parking bay outside a block of flats in Portswood Park, at the top of Bevois Hill.

The area was cordoned off, with residents not allowed in or out of the block, while police and Scenes of Crime officers, under the initial leadership of Det.Insp. Bob Duncan and Det.Sgt. Howard Kiley, examined the area. They saw that the body was curled up on a patch of grass with a piece of white plastic chain from an adjacent fence wrapped around the ankle, suggesting he had become caught up in it while trying to get away from his attacker. The body and area around it was heavily bloodstained, mainly coming from a severe throat wound. A number of footprints could be seen in the muddy ground and these were photographed, as well as plaster casts being taken. There was also a muddy footprint on the man's jeans, so this was also photographed.

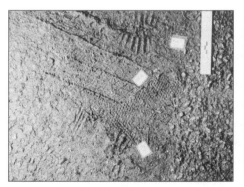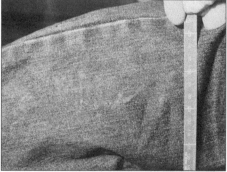

One of the footprints in mud, and the muddy footprint on the jeans. (*Hampshire Constabulary History Society*)

The parking bays opposite O'Brien's flat. (*Hampshire Constabulary History Society*)

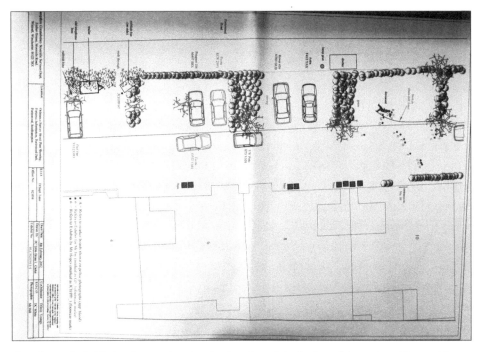

Plan, drawn by PC Brian Carter, showing the location of the body and footprints. (*Hampshire Constabulary History Society*)

Residents in the blocks of apartments along Portswood Park were questioned in the early hours of the following morning, revealing that the deceased man was Ian David O'Brien, 40, who lived in a bedsit directly opposite the parking bays.

O'Brien was a shaven-headed man, with a broken nose, who had moved into the block from his native Manchester several years ago. Neighbours said he was pleasant enough when sober, but inclined to drink heavily and become aggressive and foul mouthed. It was also known that his abusive conduct had resulted in him being barred from several public houses in the area.

A post-mortem, carried out by Home Office pathologist Dr Allen Anscombe later that day, showed that O'Brien, in addition to heavy bruising on his face and body, had sustained seven deep stabbing wounds to the head and throat, one of them with such force as to sever part of the spine and a major artery. He also had a number of deep cuts on his hands, indicating he had tried to defend himself during the attack. A fresh indented mark on his top lip suggested it was the result of a blow from somebody wearing a ring with a raised circular decoration.

As a result of enquiries in the apartment block it came to light that Thomas Jones, 56, who lived in one of the flats, had left during the night with his son, Liam James Thomas Jones, 23, and they had failed to return. Liam lived in Oxford with his mother, as his parents had separated, and frequently stayed with his father for the weekend. He was known to be unemployed and a registered drug addict who needed a daily dose of the heroin substitute methadone. It was also said that Liam wore chunky rings and other jewellery.

Police enquiries in neighbouring public houses revealed that O'Brien, who was found wearing a distinctive brown leather jacket and baseball cap, was seen on the night of the murder in the Gordon Arms, Portswood Road, in the company of a man answering the description of Liam Jones. Both men were later in the Richmond Inn, Portswood Road, where O'Brien was refused service because of his abusive behaviour. Although it was known he had cash, including banknotes, when he left the Richmond Inn that evening, no money was found on his body.

Thomas and his son returned to his flat three days later and were questioned as to their movements on the night of the murder. Liam admitted meeting O'Brien in the Gordon Arms that evening and accompanying him to the Richmond Inn, which they left together, but denied being involved in any assault. He said he had joined O'Brien in the Gordon Arms in the hope of obtaining drugs, believing that O'Brien would know where they could be obtained.

Liam and his father were detained and when they were searched a butterfly knife and small metal bar were found in a bag owned by Liam. A gold ring with a circular sovereign mounting, together with two £20 notes, were recovered from Liam and sent for forensic examination. Both men were then released on police bail.

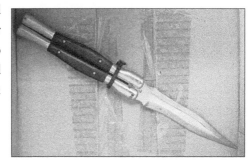

The knife found in Liam's bag. (*Hampshire Constabulary History Society*)

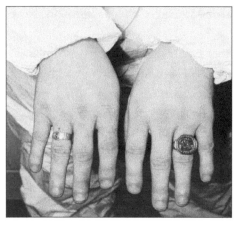 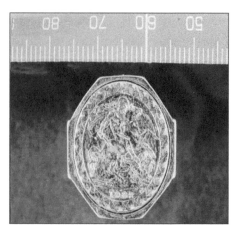

Liam's hands, wearing the ring, with a close-up of the ring. (*Hampshire Constabulary History Society*)

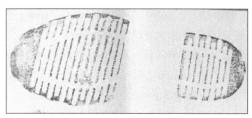 

Shoe impressions taken during the course of the investigation. (*Hampshire Constabulary History Society*)

It could not be proved beyond doubt that any matched the faint impressions at the scene.

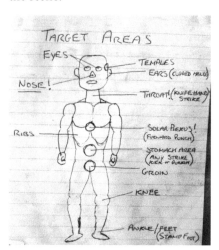

(*Hampshire Constabulary History Society*)

A search, carried out at Liam's mother's home in Oxford, resulted in a Kung Fu martial arts book found in Liam's bedroom, together with hand-drawn diagrams showing vulnerable areas of the body designated as 'targets' in an attack. These coincided with the stabbing areas found on Ian O'Brien's body. The pathologist also stated that the sovereign ring owned by Liam was identical to the circular mark found on the deceased's upper lip.

Crucially, the two £20 notes recovered from Liam bore DNA identified as that of Ian O'Brien. Both Liam and his father were therefore arrested in Oxford and brought to Southampton, where they continued to deny any involvement in O'Brien's death. Thomas said of his son 'Obviously he has said he didn't do it and I believe him. Why would he kill a piece of rubbish like that when somebody else would do it for him? It was just a matter of time. I don't get excited about characters like that; I don't even raise a sweat.'

Both men were charged, Liam with the murder of Ian O'Brien and Thomas with assisting an offender. They appeared before Judge Michael Broderick at Winchester Crown Court in December 2002, with both men pleading 'not guilty. Part of the prosecution case rested on the basis that the two had left the scene immediately after the attack in order to dispose of bloodstained clothing and the knife used to stab O'Brien. No such clothing or weapon was ever found by the police during extensive searches in both Southampton and Oxford.

In the course of the 10 day trial Liam admitted fighting with O'Brien, thus accounting for the circular mark made by his sovereign ring. He told the jury that after they left the Richmond Inn, where O'Brien had been refused service, 'I had had enough of the way he was going on. I don't remember exactly how it started but punches were thrown. I hit him round the face with my fist a few times. I remember him hitting me once. When he was on the ground I left him.' He also admitted that he had attended karate classes when he was a child and kept up a strong interest in martial arts, but said he had never been given the opportunity of putting the skills into practice.

He was then asked by Michael Parroy, the prosecuting QC, why he had not mentioned having fought with O'Brien before and he replied 'I was a junkie at the time; they are renowned for telling lies'. When asked if he had used a knife he replied 'I do not think I had one on me. I was not in the habit of carrying one.'

(This was in spite of the fact that he was carrying a 'butterfly' knife when initially detained.) He also continued to maintain that O'Brien had definitely been alive when he left him.

When asked for an explanation of O'Brien's DNA being on the two £20 notes in his possession, he said that O'Brien had sneezed when they sat in the pub together and the DNA must have got onto Liam's hands before he placed them in his jeans pockets and onto the banknotes.

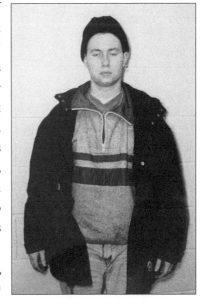

Liam James Thomas Jones. (*Hampshire Constabulary History Society***)**

On Friday 20 December 2002 at the conclusion of the trial, the judge summed up proceedings and said to the jury, 'What I want you to imagine is that you are given a box containing a number of pieces of a jigsaw puzzle. It is not much use sitting and staring at the individual pieces. What you have to do is assess them with a view to seeing which pieces fit together.'

The jury, after deliberating for over 11 hours, returned a unanimous verdict of guilty to the charge of murder and Liam was told by the judge, 'Precisely what prompted the attack on Mr O'Brien we don't know, probably only you know. It was a savage attack with severe stab wounds. I will say no more because, as you know, the sentence of murder is fixed by law, and that is life imprisonment.'

Liam's father was found not guilty of assisting an offender and was discharged from the court. Liam clapped his hands and shouted 'sweet' when that was announced.

2002 – PHILLIP TURNER – 'EVIL VOICES IN MY HEAD'

Phillip Ashley Turner, 43, who lived in a block of flats in St Denys Road, was a quiet and unassuming man who offended nobody, but one of his neighbours in a nearby flat, window cleaner Andrew Sargant, 32, had the completely unfounded fixation that Phillip was a child molester. He later said, 'evil voices in my head told me he was a paedophile'.

This fixation came to a head on the evening of Sunday 2 June 2002 when Sargant and a friend, Tony Johnson, spent the day drinking. Late that evening the pair of them, after

The block of flats in St Denys Road shared by Phillip Turner and Andrew Sargant.

drunkenly discussing Phillip's alleged sexual deviation, decided to attack him. They went to his room and without warning struck him, knocking him to the ground.

Sargant then completely lost control and, without the involvement of his friend, kicked Phillip with as much force as he could muster. The assault was so ferocious, with Sargant stamping heavily on Phillip's prone body that imprints of his trainers were subsequently found on his victim's torso. The pair then left the room.

The following afternoon Sargant met a cousin, Vanessa Haynes, at the General Hospital and said to her, 'I think I killed somebody that I kicked in the face at my flat'. He added it had happened the previous day and that the man was a paedophile. She told him he ought to hand himself in to the police.

Sargant was then contacted by a friend, Edward D'Orsey, on his mobile phone and told him he was at the General Hospital, saying, 'something has happened'. Edward joined him outside the hospital main entrance and was told, 'I've done something stupid; I think I've really hurt someone'. He added that he had been in a fight and didn't know what he had done. Edward took Sargant in his car, at about 7.15pm, and dropped him at Portswood, near traffic lights, when Sargant said he was going to hand himself in at the nearby police station.

At around 8pm Sargant phoned his father and said he had killed a man who lived in the same flat as him, the man was a paedophile who messed around with children. He said he had got into a fight the previous night and had gone back earlier today and found him with blood coming from his mouth and that he was cold and dead.

At 8.15pm he went to Portswood police station and told the enquiry officer, Patricia Cole, that he had been involved in a serious assault the previous night and had left the man in a bad state, bleeding from his ears and mouth. She asked him why he hadn't called an ambulance and he replied that he was very drunk.

He was taken to the house in St Denys Road by PC Roberts and they were joined by paramedics Andre Pilling and Caroline Thompson, who together with Sargant, were admitted by a resident, Andrew Hayes. Sargant took them to a ground floor flat where they saw Phillip Turner lying on the floor in a foetal position with dried blood coming from his left ear.

Mr Pilling said that the man was dead and it appeared, from the nature of his injuries, that he had been kicked. Sargant then said words to the effect that 'Yeah, me and another bloke gave him a good kicking last night'. He added that the man was a paedophile and had assaulted two three-year-old girls. They all went outside and Mr Pilling repeated what Sargant had said, in his presence. PC Roberts then cautioned Sargant and arrested him on suspicion of murder. Sargant, who was very calm, then said, 'He's a nonce, we gave him a kicking.'

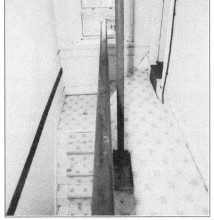

The stairway of the flats in St Denys Road, with blood marks marked by small tags.
(*Hampshire Constabulary History Society*)

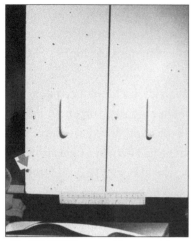

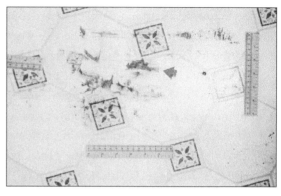

A blood spattered cupboard and bloody footprints on the kitchen floor. (*Hampshire Constabulary History Society*)

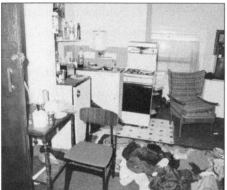

Views of the kitchen (left) and bedroom (right) of Phillip Turner's flat. (*Hampshire Constabulary History Society*)

Sargant was taken to Southampton Central police station and a murder investigation opened, given the codename Operation Erindale.

Sargant was interviewed on Tuesday 4 June by DC Zacharias and said that the other man involved was fellow resident Tony Johnson, who was also arrested. Johnson, at Bitterne police station, said, 'As it happens, I tried to break it up.'

Sargant said he had been drinking vodka with Johnson, who was the first to hit Turner, but admitted that he had kicked him several times to the head and shoulders, leaving him lying on the floor. He said he had struck other residents in the past and suffered from 'vodka fuelled violence'. During the course of his interview he said, 'Evil voices in my head told me he was a paedophile and to kill him. I had been given the right to do so by God.' He also said that the main voice in his head was called Humphrey, who had been with him since childhood, but only recently had he started to tell him to hurt people.

At 11pm that night Sargant was taken to the General Hospital for an emergency hernia operation, returning to custody in the morning of Monday 10 June. When further interviewed he stated that when he said he blacked out he meant he loses track of what is going on. The night of the attack he woke up to find he was kicking and stamping on Turner, who was on his hands and knees, but was unable to say why he did it.

A post-mortem carried out by Home Office pathologist Dr Alan Anscombe, found multiple injuries to Turner's head, chest and arms, with patterns of footwear, consistent with being kicked and stamped on. He had 10 broken ribs and a crushing injury to his voice box that could have been instantly fatal. There was no fracture of the skull.

Sargant was charged with the murder of Phillip Turner and appeared before the Honourable Mr Justice Nelson at Winchester Crown Court on Monday 1 November 2004. He admitted carrying out the attack but denied it was murder.

The defence called consultant psychiatrist Dr Gwilym Hayes, who told the court that Sargant's mental state fluctuated from one minute to the next. It meant that it was difficult to discover the illness that Sargant was suffering from and to know just how ill he was at the time of the attack.

He told the jury, 'I believe he was suffering from a mental illness at that moment in time, and that illness is schizophrenia.' The prosecution, however, put to the jury that excess alcohol was the prime factor in the assault.

Although Sargant's counsel asked the jury to find that the crime was committed when Sargant was suffering from diminished responsibility, the jury of five women and seven men unanimously rejected this claim and found him guilty of murder.

The judge told Sargant, 'Phillip Turner suffered a terribly cruel death. He was targeted because of your perceived view of his sexual behaviour, which had no basis of truth. You are an extremely dangerous and deluded man.

You pose a risk to anyone you consider to be a homosexual or paedophile. Although

the guidelines suggest a starting point of 15 years for your life sentence, I am increasing it because of the aggravating feature of the violence and recommend that you serve at least 20 years.'

Sargant showed no emotion as he was led from the dock by five nurses from Broadmoor High Security Mental Hospital, where he was to be detained.

The unfortunate Phillip Turner was cremated prior to the trial.

Left: Andrew Sargant. (*Hampshire Constabulary History Society*)

2002 – SHAH WAHAB – A SINGLE BLOW

At around 1.10am on Tuesday 3 September 2002 Shah Abdul Wahab, 38, a bachelor and restaurant worker, was standing outside Brannigan's public house in the High Street. He had just left the premises and was about to make his way home to Cranbury Avenue.

Brannigan's, where 'cavorting' was encouraged, just after it closed in 2007.

Bystanders saw a man suddenly approach Shah Wahab and, without warning, strike him a single blow in the face, knocking him to the pavement. As he fell Shah's head struck the pavement very heavily and he immediately became unconscious, with obvious severe head injuries. The man, who was about 5ft 3in tall, with short blonde hair and wearing a white shirt, calmly walked away and was seen to go down East Street.

Following a '999' call the unconscious Shah was taken by ambulance to the General Hospital and police at the scene interviewed a number of witnesses. Immediate enquiries were headed by Det.Sgt Robert Bowness.

Shah underwent a four-hour operation to remove a blood clot from his brain but his condition remained critical, with his family maintaining a bedside vigil. Although on a life support machine, Shah's condition deteriorated and following consultation with his family the machine was switched off. The assault had now become a murder enquiry, with the code name Operation Whitegate, led by Det.Insp. Jason Hogg.

Publicity was given in the *Southern Daily Echo*, with his sister, Mrs Mona Khatun, appealing for witnesses to come forward, saying her brother was 'a caring, lovely person'.

Mention was also made of the fact that the police were examining CCTV footage taken in the High Street and East Street areas. They were particularly keen to speak to any men who were in the area wearing white shirts and appealed for them to come forward to be eliminated.

Two days after the assault, construction worker Andrew, 28, of Wavell Road, Bitterne, walked into Central police station and admitted that he was the person who had thrown the punch. He said he had gone to Brannigan's with friends to celebrate his birthday and claimed that Wahab had touched his backside and winked at him outside the public house. Andrew stated that after throwing the punch he had joined his friends to get a taxi and only realised how badly he had injured Mr Wahab when he heard it on the news the following day.

He was charged with the murder and appeared before Mr Justice Michael Brodrick at Winchester Crown Court on Thursday 9 January 2003, when he pleaded guilty to manslaughter.

The judge said, 'I have the unenviable task of having to pass a sentence which satisfies both sides of the public gallery. In my view that is impossible. The strong likelihood is that I will satisfy neither.'

He then said to Andrew, 'What happened was undoubtedly a quite unnecessary over-reaction to what you perceived to be an unwelcome approach from the deceased. But you could, and should, have let it pass and go on your way. The indications are also that it wasn't a particularly hard punch.'

Andrew was then sentenced to 12 months imprisonment.

Shah Wahab is buried in Hollybrook Cemetery in plot D8-296 and the English inscription, underneath Arabic lettering, reads:

SHAH ABDUL WAHAB
(SHAH JALAL)
03.09.02
AGED 37

2003 – MOHAMMED ALI – ASSAULT ON AN ASYLUM SEEKER

Mohammed Isa Hassan Ali, 22, fled his native town of Kabul in Afghanistan in 2001, entering the UK as an asylum seeker at Dover on 13 June that year. A Shi'ite Muslim, he had been abducted by the Taliban and brutally tortured, leaving him with the loss of sight in one eye and heavy scarring on his back. Initially settling in Newcastle, he moved to Southampton in October 2002 and obtained lodging with several other asylum seekers, sharing a three-bedroom mid-terraced multi-occupancy house in Ancasta Road, Bevois Valley. Although partially disabled, as a result of his battering from the Taliban, he nevertheless managed to find low paid employment locally picking mushrooms, and on a production line with a fruit and vegetable packing company.

At about 10pm on Saturday 8 February 2003, Mohammed left the house, telling his housemates he intended going to the city centre. He returned home at 2am with a blood-stained head injury, and told them he had been attacked by a group of British lads who hit him on the head with a bottle.

He then went to his bed and remained there throughout the following Sunday, saying he felt sick and giddy and had a severe headache, but at 1pm on Monday a fellow occupant checked on him and found him unconscious. An ambulance was called but the ambulance crew, Gareth Ray and Dean Pearce, together with paramedic Simon Fairburn, were unable to rouse him. PS McMann arrived at 1.40pm and

Mohammed's shared home in Ancasta Road.

was told by the paramedic that Ali could die. He therefore travelled with him in the ambulance and he was taken direct to the General Hospital, where Ali was treated by the emergency resuscitation team but life was pronounced extinct at 2pm.

A murder investigation then began, with the codename Operation Brindle, under the command of Det.Supt Alan Betts. A post-mortem by Dr Anscombe confirmed that death was due to brain damage and a fractured skull brought about by a massive blow to the back of the head. He also had a bruise on the right side of his head. It was therefore suspected that the deceased had been struck with something like a bottle or other heavy object. Ali was found to weigh only 9 stone 8 pounds.

MURDER POLICE APPEAL

On Saturday 8th February 2003 Mohammed Isa Hasan Ali was fatally assaulted by a number of persons in the city centre.

Did you see Hasan Ali on Saturday night? Did you see this assault?

Can you assist police in any way with information about this incident?

If so contact the incident room in Southampton on

023 8059 9832 or 0845 045 4545

or call free on Crimestoppers on

0800 555111

Poster circulated and published in the media. (*Hampshire Constabulary History Society*)

Detectives carried out house-to-house enquiries in the area and CCTV footage from cameras in the city centre were seized to see if Mohammed's movements could be traced. A photograph of the deceased was found at his home and this was circulated to the media with an appeal for information.

As a direct result of this appeal, Alex, 21, a 17-stone former rugby player and bus driver in Oxford, phoned the Hampshire police control room from his home in Oxford at 8.14pm on Friday 14 February. He gave his address and telephone number and said he had been in Southampton that Saturday night and believed he might have been involved. He had been in Southampton with his girlfriend and a group of friends, celebrating the birthday of two of them. Alex said that police officers had attended when he was involved in an incident with a man outside the Nationwide Building Society at the top of New Road. He said he could not recall it but the others in the group had told him the man's photograph was shown in a poster circulated by the police.

The former Nationwide Building Society building at Above Bar/New Road.

The police control room tape and recovered CCTV footage was searched and it was found that the incident was the subject of a '999' call at 1.45am on Sunday 9 February. It had been recorded on both the Council CCTV and one from within the Nationwide Building Society and Alex had been the subject of a check by PC Thomas O'Grady and Special Constable Rodney Fitch.

The officers had found Ali sitting on the pavement but communication had been impossible because of the language barrier. Ali had no apparent injury, there was no blood and he was walking normally. Alex identified himself to the officers, saying he was in the process of applying to join the Hampshire Constabulary and had merely pushed Ali over. The ambulance crew arrived but there appeared to be no reason to take any action and Ali walked away.

The CCTV footage showed Mohammed being pushed very forcibly, with two hands, by a man outside the Nationwide Building Society building at the junction of Above Bar and New Road in the early hours of Sunday 9 February. The push was extremely violent, resulting in Mohammed falling backwards, completely without control. The videos, however, were of poor quality.

One of the stills from the council CCTV video, showing Ali being helped by one of the group after the assault. (*Hampshire Constabulary History Society*)

Initially the links between this incident and Mohammed Ali had not been identified because of Ali's account of being struck on the head with a bottle by a group of men. Intensive enquiries were made, with CCTV footage thoroughly checked and records of other incidents in the city that night checked, in case there had been a further incident involving Ali, but there was no evidence of such an event.

Other members of the group were interviewed and said they saw Alex grab hold of Ali by his jacket lapels, throwing rather than pushing him, towards the railings. Ali's head hit the top of the railings, on the side of his head, and he landed flat on his back on the pavement, striking the back of his head heavily as he did so. Some of the group were student nurses but when they went to assist found he could sit up unassisted.

It was revealed that Alex had an argument with his girlfriend in the Walkabout Bar and this continued after they left and were walking along the High Street. One of the party, Ian King, tried to speak to Alex to calm him down, but he responded aggressively and headbutted Mr King, but without any real force. It was just after this that the group arrived at the Nationwide Building Society, where Ali was standing. Alex had said, aggressively, to Ali, 'What are you looking at?' before he threw him by the lapels.

Alex was arrested at 1.15pm on Sunday 16 February at his home by DC Roger Lattimore on suspicion of murder. When cautioned he made no reply. He was taken to Alton police station and questioned by DC Woodward and DC Case.

Alex said he had drunk in the region of 13 pints of beer on the night in question. He had quarrelled with his girlfriend, Sarah James, and told the police that as he walked past Mohammed Ali, who was leaning on a lamp post outside the Nationwide building, 'He said something and laughed. I couldn't understand what he was saying and thought

his words were directed at Sarah or both of us. When he leant forward I just pushed him away. I didn't want him to fall over; I just wanted him to move out of the way.'

However, the CCTV camera showed that the push, with both hands, was violent, and Mohammed had fallen with both hands in his pockets, thus unable to stop the back of his head striking the pavement and/or the railings. It also showed that Alex was almost twice the

The spot where Mohammed Ali fell and thought to have struck his head on the railings before falling to the pavement. (*Hampshire Constabulary History Society*)

size of Mohammed. As the camera clearly showed no justification for the assault, he was charged by DC Woodward at Alton police station at 10.45pm the following day with manslaughter and released on bail.

He appeared before Judge Michael Broderick at Winchester Crown Court in early December 2003, and pleaded 'not guilty'. In the course of the trial he claimed he thought Mohammed was about to touch his girlfriend when he pushed him out of the way. He said he feared for her safety, but the CCTV showed no evidence of this. He also stated he had broken down in tears when he saw the man was unconscious.

At the conclusion of the two-week trial the jury found him guilty of manslaughter and Judge Broderick told Alex, 'This case is a tragedy for you because you were a man without convictions until now. But equally this case is a tragedy for Mr Ali, who was minding his own business and lost his life because of your actions. You will go to prison

for 18 months.'

Prior to the trial the police contacted the Afghanistan embassy to trace Mohammed Ali's relatives and his mother was found. A campaign was launched to raise funds to fly his body home for burial, but this was stopped when his mother became ill.

Instead a memorial service took place to commemorate his life and a tree, dedicated to him, was planted in Eastpark, close to the Nationwide Building Society, and he was buried in Fareham.

2003 – RICHARD KELLY – STABBED IN THE STREET

Just before 9am on Tuesday 17 June 2003, Richard Patrick Kelly, 32, living in Orchard House, Orchard Lane, was walking with friends along St Mary Street, Chapel, near the junction with Craven Street.

At the same time Derek Irvine-Neary, 37, who lived in nearby Northam Road, came out of the post office on the opposite side of the road, where he had just collected his benefit money. He saw Kelly and remembered that about eight weeks earlier he had been involved in a dispute with a drunken and aggressive Kelly outside his home in Northam Road. In the course of the argument Kelly had threatened him, but it had come to nothing.

Upper St Mary Street, the scene where Richard Kelly was walking with friends.

At this second meeting Irvine-Neary crossed the road and started to argue with Kelly, which turned into some general pushing and shoving. This became violent, in the course of which Irvine-Neary pulled out a padlock and chain from his pocket and swung it around towards Kelly's head, but without striking him.

Kelly's friends then managed to calm the situation and Kelly sat on the ground before getting up and offering his hand to Irvine-Neary, saying, 'Let's forget it'.

However, Irvine-Neary then produced a knife, with which he stabbed Kelly in the stomach.

As he did so, Robert Brownsea, who was cycling along the street, saw the struggle and heard someone mention a knife. With no thought for his safety he got off his cycle and placed himself between the two men in an attempt to calm them, noticing as he did so that Irvine-Neary was holding a small kitchen knife in his hand.

Kelly then collapsed to the pavement, bleeding from his abdomen and Irvine-Neary walked away. However, he was pursued by Robert Brownsea, who took the knife from him, dropping it to the ground, and forcibly restrained him while others phoned for the police. Both ambulance and police rapidly arrived on the scene and Kelly was rushed to hospital in a critical condition.

Irvine-Neary was detained and taken to Southampton Central police station and the area of the attack sealed off with tape from Johnson Street to Clifford Street.

Richard Kelly died shortly after admission to hospital, the cause of death stated to be 'catastrophic bleeding from a v-shaped slit, 14 cm deep, in his abdomen'. This depth

The official police photograph of the cordoned-off street, with scenes of crime officers grouped in the distance, at the scene of the attack. (*Hampshire Constabulary History Society*)

Aerial view of the murder area. (*Hampshire Constabulary History Society*)

The scene of the attack. (*Hampshire Constabulary History Society*)

was later confirmed to be slightly longer than the length of the knife blade found at the scene.

An immediate murder enquiry was launched, with the codename Operation Conna, under the control of Det.Ch.Insp. Dean Jones, with Derek Irvine-Neary subsequently charged with murder.

Derek Irvine-Neary appeared before Judge Michael Brodrick at Winchester Crown Court on 22 June 2004, where he pleaded guilty to the murder of Richard Kelly. By this time the unfortunate Richard had been cremated.

Irvine-Neary was remanded for reports and re-appeared on 29 July when he was sentenced to life imprisonment with a minimum of 11 years to be served before becoming eligible for parole. Because of the time already spent in custody he would actually serve a minimum of nine years and 11 months.

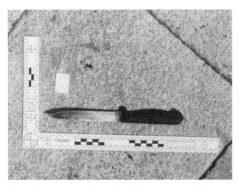
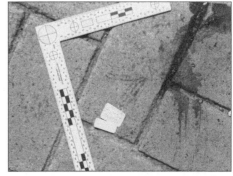

The bloodstained knife at the scene and bloodstains on the pavement. (*Hampshire Constabulary History Society*)

2003 – ALEC NEWMAN – THE BBQ MURDER

At around 1am on Good Friday, 18 April 2003, Steven Hanley, a student, was woken in his Denzil Avenue, Newtown, flat by the sounds of what appeared to be violent fighting in the flat above, occupied by Robert Craig, 44. He heard the sound of moaning and somebody saying, 'Leave him or you'll do 15 years for murder'. This frightened him, so he climbed out of his ground floor window and ran to a nearby friend's house, from where he called the police.

Sgt Brendon Close and other officers arrived and found Stephen Newton, 52, slumped outside the building, bleeding from severe injuries to his face and body. The sergeant entered Robert Craig's flat, where he found fresh blood on the floor. Craig denied having been involved in a fight but said he knew that Newton had been beaten with copper poles and wooden sticks studded with blades. He then said, 'You will find a body around the corner in Cranbury Avenue'.

The officers followed his directions and found the dead body of a man lying on a secluded path just around the corner. It was that of Alec Leslie Newman, 50, a divorcee from St Marks. They then followed a trail of blood that led from the body to the Cranbury Avenue flat of Thomas Davies, 45, which he shared with Stephen Newton. Inside was Davies, with his then partner, Cheryl Heys, 39, of Bourne Road, Shirley.

Alec Newman's body was clearly badly injured, with a subsequent post-mortem by Dr Alan Anscombe showing he had sustained six broken ribs, four of which had been fractured in at least two places, and severe bruising to the head and stomach, consistent with him having been punched and kicked a number of times. The laceration to his head was so deep that his skull could be seen.

There were internal injuries to his stomach which the doctor stated were probably caused by someone stamping on his abdomen at least twice while he was lying on his back. The serious injuries were the cause of death.

Questioning of the four, who were described as part of a community of long-term alcoholics, revealed that they had all taken part in a BBQ at Craig's flat in Denzil Avenue earlier that evening, later returning to the Cranbury Avenue flat of Davies and Newton. All four were detained and taken to the Civic Centre police station for further questioning.

Their clothing was taken for forensic examination, carried out by forensic scientist Stephen Harrington. He found bloodstains on the clothing of Thomas Davies and his partner Cheryl Heys, confirmed by DNA testing as that of the deceased, Alec Newman. He also found Mr Newman's blood on Robert Craig's shoes.

The apartments in Cranbury Avenue, occupied by Thomas Davies and Stephen Newton.

Thomas Davies, however, told detectives that Stephen Newton had battered Alec Newman to death and then dumped his body in the secluded alleyway outside the flat. He made a recorded statement in which he said that trouble had arisen in the flat because Alec Newman started to touch Cheryl. He went on, 'I slapped him and flung him out of the front door. Steve Newton went after him, saying ,'You're a nonce. I'm going to kill you. I'm going to stab the nonce.'

Davies said he and Cheryl then left and went to a flat in Denzil Avenue. Newton arrived and admitted he had killed Mr Newman. Davies then told the police 'Me and Cheryl didn't know what to do. We panicked. We went back to Cranbury Avenue and checked Alec. He was just lying there. Then the police turned up.'

The remaining three all disputed Davies' account, stating they played no part in the assault on Alec Newman, who had subsequently been cremated.

All four were jointly charged with the murder of Alec Newman and appeared before Mr Justice Owen at Winchester Crown Court on Friday 25 June 2004. He directed the jury to find Stephen Newton and Cheryl Heys not guilty, based on the lack of evidence against them.

Robert Craig and Thomas Davies were remanded to face trial at a later date and when their case was dealt with, the second jury found Robert Craig not guilty but convicted Thomas Davies, who was sentenced to life imprisonment.

A twist to the tale came at a subsequent inquest on Tuesday 2 November 2004. Robert Craig's body was found, fully clothed, floating next to a pontoon at Saxon Wharf in the River Itchen at 8.15am Thursday 2 September, a month after his acquittal for Alec Newman's murder.

The inquest jury heard that Mr Craig, rather than use a dinghy, would often swim out to the small boat he owned moored in the river. It therefore appeared that he had got into difficulty. A post-mortem had revealed he had only drunk the equivalent of two pints of beer before getting into the water. The police investigation did not reveal anything suspicious about his drowning and did not believe that he had committed suicide by jumping from the nearby Itchen Bridge.

Records show that Thomas Davies also died, in HM Prison, Swayleside, on 11 September 2007, so the two key participants are no longer with us.

2005 – NOKUKHANYA MKHONTA – AN IRRATIONAL JEALOUSY

Jose Pedro. (*Hampshire Constabulary History Society*)

Nokukhanya Faith Mkhonta, 20, a Swaziland-born nursing home carer, lived with her boyfriend, Jose Pedro, 23, a native of Angola, in a bedsit in Exmoor Road. Miss Mkhonta worked as a carer in a nursing home in Totton and was sending money back to Swaziland to help fund her brother and sister's education. Her family described her as 'a loving, caring, responsible and outgoing girl, always full of cheer and smiles all the time'.

Jose Pedro was also of good character. He was a talented student, an Angolan junior chess champion, who had come to Britain in 2002 to study accounting at the Southampton City College. He was said to be 'a normal, mild-mannered man, with impeccable manners, a considerate, kind and a loving son'.

However, Pedro had developed an unfounded delusion that Nokukhanya was being unfaithful. On 15 December 2005, following a works Christmas party, he thought she had cheated on him with a work colleague and attacked her. He punched her several times, threw a chair at her, cut off some of her hair and cut up her clothes. He then passed over her mobile phone and said ,'If you want to phone your Mum you should do it now because tonight I'm going to kill you.' Neighbours, hearing the loud disturbance, called the police, who arrested and charged him with assault. He was then bailed to appear at court at a later date, on condition he was not to contact Ms Mkhonta directly or indirectly.

The Exmoor Road bedsit.

Ms Mkhonta was provided with alternative accommodation but decided to return to her Exmoor Road home and stay with a friend in another bedsit on the ground floor.

However, at 1.30pm on 22 December smoke was seen coming from the two top windows of the house in Exmoor Road by two builders, Richard Cullen and Ainslie Ateyo, who were working nearby.

Mr Cullen ran over to the house and banged on the front door, to warn the occupants, while Mr Ateyo called the emergency services.

The occupant of the ground floor flat, Abdul Karimi, looked out of his window and was warned of the fire by Mr Cullen. Mr Karimi opened the door to his room, leading to the front hallway, and saw smoke and Jose Pedro standing at the bottom of the stairs.

Mr Karimi left the house, telling the builders that there was somebody inside. Mr Ateyo tried to open the front door but it was forcibly slammed shut against him by Pedro.

The fire brigade attended just before 1.50pm and forced an entry into the house. Firefighter Green, while searching the ground floor, saw Pedro on the ground in a narrow pathway outside the building. The firefighters and paramedics found he was suffering severe burns to his side, deep cuts to the fingers of his right hand and a head injury.

He was therefore taken to the Southampton General Hospital, where it was found that he was drunk, with his condition the equivalent of two and half times over the drink-driving limit.

The cutway where Pedro was found, underneath the open bathroom window. (*Hampshire Constabulary History Society*)

On continuing the search of the building, Firefighter White found Nokukhanya Mkhonta lying on her back in the ground floor room, next to a burnt out bed where the fire had started. She was dragged outside backwards and attended to by paramedic Wensley-Smith, who noticed a wound to her left breast. He attempted to treat her but life was pronounced extinct at 2.15pm.

The burnt-out bed in the ground floor room where the fire started. (*Hampshire Constabulary History Society*)

Firefighters continued to search the building and Firefighter House forced an entry to a locked bathroom on the first floor. He saw that the bathroom window, above where Pedro had been found, had been completely smashed and there was blood on the sink and wall.

A subsequent post-mortem revealed she had sustained multiple stab wounds, four to the chest and 23 to her back, with the tip of a knife broken off inside her body. There was no smoke or fire damage to her airways and the cause of death was given as multiple stab wounds.

The smashed bathroom window that Pedro climbed through. (*Hampshire Constabulary History Society*)

A forensic examination of the house confirmed that the fire had started in the area of the corner of the bed and that there were a number of blood markings throughout the premises. A bloodstained knife was recovered from the room where the fire had started and where Ms Mkhonta had been found, and the blood was later confirmed as belonging to both Pedro and Ms Mkhonta.

The bloodstained knife with a broken tip, and the tip recovered from Mkhonta's body. (*Hampshire Constabulary History Society*)

Rear side door with blood marks around the handle. (*Hampshire Constabulary History Society*)

Smoke damaged areas on the first floor. (*Hampshire Constabulary History Society*)

Following Pedro's hospital treatment he was discharged on Friday 6 January and arrested by DC Powell-Hills on suspicion of the murder of Nokukhanya Mkhonta and arson with intent to endanger life. He was later taken to Lyndhurst police station and questioned in the presence of his solicitor.

He admitted having stabbed his girlfriend and setting fire to the flat, stating that after seeing Ms Mkhonta with another man on 14 December he decided to kill both her and himself. He stabbed her many times when she was in the ground floor room, before dousing himself and the bed with cooking oil.

He then set both bed and himself alight, in an attempt to kill himself, but because of the pain left the room. He then went up into the bathroom on the first floor and tried to fracture his skull by hitting it on the sink. When this proved impossible, he smashed the bathroom window and jumped out of the window, believing that this would kill him.

He was subsequently charged with both arson and murder and stood trial at Winchester Crown Court in February 2007. However, on 23 February the girl's mother launched into a sustained verbal attack from the public gallery and the trial had to be abandoned. Pedro was sent to hospital, suffering from severe psychotic depression, but was deemed fit enough to stand trial again on 2 June.

He appeared before Judge Guy Boney QC, and pleaded guilty to manslaughter on the grounds of diminished responsibility. Oba Nsugbe QC, defending Pedro, said although it is a complicated diagnosis, doctors agree there was psychotic depression. The judge then made an interim order under the Mental Health Act to remand Pedro into custody at Ravenswood House, near Fareham, for a case conference involving doctors and psychiatrists to meet in September. The judge would then make a decision at a later date once he knew what the mental health position was.

The case was brought before the court again on 8 January 2008, when consultant psychiatrist Jan Vermeulen told the court that Pedro 'remained in an extremely fragile mental state. The more pressing risk is a risk to himself rather than others. I am a bit concerned whether a prison sentence would minimise the possibility that morbid jealousy will recur in a future relationship.'

The judge said, 'The dreadful truth is your irrational and growing jealousy slowly destroyed your relationship and the love she had for you. As the relationship deteriorated, so did your treatment of her. The final assault was preceded by escalating threats of violence and assaults of increasing severity.'

He added that all the doctors conclude that while Pedro probably suffered from a personality disorder it is not a condition that requires psychiatric treatment in a hospital. The judge said 'Given that the choice in this kind of situation has to be between a hospital order or a prison sentence, and a hospital order is not an option open to this

court, these are all considerations which bear on the length of the prison sentence which should be imposed.'

As Pedro had already served two years on remand, he then sentenced him to four and a half years imprisonment, leaving less than two years to be served, together with a recommendation that he be deported at the end of his sentence. Pedro was, in fact, deported to Angola on 1 June 2008, with no permission to enter the UK again for 10 years.

Jose Pedro after his arrest. (*Hampshire Constabulary History Society***)**

2006 – PETER RAMSEY – A 'HAPPY-SLAPPY' KILLING

Canadian-born Peter Ramsey, 40, an artist, lived in Green Park Road, Millbrook, with his partner Victoria Lewis, and during 2006 they were both subjected to harassment from local youths, all of which had been reported to the police.

At around 6.30pm on Tuesday 10 October 2006 they left home and walked to the nearby Tesco Express to buy some provisions. While inside a group of local youths started to harass Peter, one of them flicking Peter's nose and another grabbing his jacket.

Peter went outside and remonstrated with them and the group left him to walk around the corner into Pennine Road. The couple then walked into Green Park Road and were followed by the same group, who had returned. Some of them started throwing stones at the couple and one shouted, 'Do you want a fight?' Another shouted out about Peter's long hair, saying it was greasy and lanky.

Peter Charles Ramsey. (*Hampshire Constabulary History Society*)

One of the youths then slapped Peter in the face and walked away, while another went up and punched him in the face, whereupon he fell to the ground, striking his head on the kerb in the process. He was helped up by Victoria and a passer-by and returned home, where he complained of feeling unwell.

A short time later Victoria found him on the bedroom floor, unable to stand or talk. She called for an ambulance and he was taken to the General Hospital where he needed two operations to remove blood clots from his brain. His condition was said to be critical and the police started a serious crime investigation under the codename Operation Apiary. Peter, who never regained consciousness and became 'brain dead', died three days later when his life support was turned off with the agreement of his partner. It then became a murder investigation.

One 13-year-old boy went to Shirley police station with his mother the following morning to admit being involved in the incident. The attendance was at her instigation after her son had told her what happened.

The Tesco Express video had been seized by the police and this showed the youths outside the store and following the harassed couple. They were soon identified and enquiries traced a further five of those involved, all of whom were detained. (Although names of all those involved are known, they cannot be published because of their ages, ranging from 13 to 15, and subsequent court restrictions.)

When they were interviewed at Bitterne police station, under the stipulated conditions of other adults being present and the length of interview, it was revealed that the group had earlier discussed carrying out a 'happy-slappy' on Peter. This is a term which refers to an assault that is videoed by others, usually on mobile phones, to be later circulated to others as a form of amusement. One of the youths already had a

Stills from the store video given in evidence. (*Hampshire Constabulary History Society*)

conviction for a robbery where the victim was filmed on a camera phone while being beaten. One of the boys had filmed the attack on Peter Ramsey but as the picture was of poor quality he deleted it.

As a result of the interviews with the five boys and one girl arrested, two 15-year-old boys and a 13-year-old boy were jointly charged with manslaughter. They appeared before Judge Guy Boney QC at Winchester Crown Court on 8 December 2006, when one of the 15-year-olds pleaded guilty to the manslaughter of Peter Ramsey.

The proceedings were adjourned to January, for the 15-year-old to be sentenced and the case heard against the remaining two boys. The 15-year-old who had pleaded guilty, and the 13-year-old, were both remanded in custody, the remaining 15-year-old was granted conditional bail. When the three reappeared before the court on 18 January 2007, the 13-year-old also pleaded guilty to the manslaughter of Peter Ramsey. He was one of the youngest persons in the country to plead guilty to such a charge and his mother and grandmother sat weeping in the court as he did so.

The case was again adjourned to 15 March for the trial of the remaining 15-year-old to take place and the other two to be sentenced. However, there was a dramatic turn of events when the case against the 15-year-old, who had pleaded 'not guilty', was dropped.

Justin Gau, the prosecuting counsel, told the judge that the only evidence against the 15-year-old was that of a young man who was present during the incident. He then said, 'Matters were passed to me for my observations, just a week ago, in relation to the issues surrounding this witness. I take the view that his credibility was seriously compromised and accordingly take the view that there was not sufficient evidence in this case so that a jury could properly convict the defendant. I take the view that no evidence should be offered against the defendant.'

The boy's defending counsel, Stewart Jones QC, then said he would have been attacking the witness's motives and his veracity and asked that a verdict of not guilty be entered and the boy discharged. Mr Justice Jack, the new presiding judge, did just that and the unnamed youth walked free from the court. The facts mentioned were not explained in open court.

The case against the remaining 13 and 15-year-old boys was then adjourned for pre-sentence reports. They appeared again in June 2007, when one, then aged 14, was sentenced to two and a half years detention and the other, then aged 16, to three years detention. Both, however, because of time spent in custody, only had to spend half of the sentences.

2007 – REM AROYAN – DEATH OF A VIOLENT STEPFATHER

The evening of Sunday 20 May 2007 was a happy one for Rem Aroyan, who was celebrating his 51st birthday. Born in the former Soviet republic of Latvia in 1956, he had come to the UK as an asylum seeker in 2000, leaving behind his partner Tamara and her son Andrejs. He told the UK immigration authorities he had been attacked in Armenia following his employment with a politician who had been murdered by his opponents, but his claim for asylum was initially rejected. After it was upheld on appeal he settled in Southampton, where he obtained work as a construction site driver. It is, however, believed with good reasons that he was, in fact, a Latvian subject named Robert Arutjunans, but this cannot be confirmed.

Trinity Court, Freemantle.

Tamara Hohlova came from her native Latvia and joined Rem Aroyan in late 2006 at Southampton, where they married in January 2007. Her son, Andrejs Hohlovs, 22 (the different final letter of the surname is correct) had arrived in the UK in December 2005 and lived on his own until he joined his mother in 2006. Tamara, 44, obtained work as a part-time cleaner and her son Andrejs, became a croupier at the Harbour House Casino at the Town Quay.

Rem, Tamara's second husband, had boasted to her that he had served a sentence in a Georgian prison in the 1970s after knifing a man and gave every indication that he was prone to use violence. The family then became tenants of a first-floor privately rented flat at Trinity Court, Paynes Road.

During the evening's celebrations at the flat, where they were joined by several friends, Rem Aroyan, although very drunk, decided to drive to Ocean Village, against the pleas of his wife and stepson. He returned after midnight, even more drunk, and a violent argument with Andrejs then developed in his stepson's bedroom, in the course of which Rem attacked Andrejs, punching him on the head and body.

The two men fell onto the bed and Tamara, in her nightclothes, came into the room and tried to force them apart, but without success. Andrejs managed to break away and fearing he would again be attacked ,grabbed a large knife that was in the room to defend himself. Rem got off the bed and Andrejs initially struck him on the head with the butt of the knife, but when this failed to stop Rem he continued to punch him and then started to stab him.

The end result was that Rem sustained a total of 16 stab wounds, several in the neck, as well as 21 severe bruises. He then fell down, in a pool of blood, coming mainly from

Bloodstained light switch and door handle in the Trinity Court flat. (*Hampshire Constabulary History Society*)

Heavily bloodstained floor where the deceased had collapsed. (*Hampshire Constabulary History Society*)

The knife that was taken from Andrejs. (*Hampshire Constabulary History Society*)

his neck, with his wife desperately cradling him in her arms. He said to his wife, 'Can you see what he has done?' and then collapsed.

Tamara took off her pyjama bottoms and pressed them against the wound to stem the flow of blood. Andrejs ran from the flat as an ambulance was called at 00.56am, but despite the intense efforts of paramedic Shane Woolmore, Rem died on the floor of the bedroom.

The flat had now become a murder scene, given the code name Operation Terrington, and the police who attended, including Det.Supt Betts and Det.Insp. Brown, quickly organised the cordoning off of the block of 18 flats while scenes of crime officers carried out a detailed fingertip search.

Andrejs, in the meantime, had gone to a nearby friend's house, where he cleaned himself before returning to the flat, where he saw Det.Supt Betts and DI Brown and said, 'I am the one you want'.

DI Brown noticed that Andrejs' light-coloured trousers were heavily bloodstained and arrested him on suspicion of murder. Andrejs replied, 'Can I ask one question, is everyone all right?' The officer then removed a knife from Andrejs' pocket.

Andrejs Hohlovs was taken to Lyndhurst police station where he was questioned by DC Cutting and DC Travers on 21 May, in the presence of his solicitor and interpreters. He answered 'no comment' to all questions.

A post-mortem was carried out on Rem Aroyan by Home Office pathologist Dr Hugh White, who found deep lacerations to the outside of the upper left leg, behind the left armpit, front left of chest, arms, top and left of skull and one going through behind the left ear and down into the neck. The cause of death was given as multiple incised wounds and he was subsequently cremated.

Andrejs was charged on 22 May with the murder of his stepfather and appeared before Judge Guy Boney QC at Winchester Crown Court on 2 November 2007, when he pleaded 'not guilty' on the basis that he had only defended himself against Rem. By this time Rem Aroyan had been cremated. After an eight-day trial the six-man and six-woman jury deliberated for six hours to arrive at a unanimous verdict of not guilty to murder but guilty of manslaughter, deciding that Andrejs had not intended to kill Rem.

The judge then adjourned the case for pre-sentence reports, and when Andrejs re-appeared before him on Wednesday 12 December 2007, the judge said he was prepared to take the view that Rem Aroyan had instigated the violence and that the first blows were made with the butt of the knife, which was simply the closest thing to hand. He also said, 'The remorse you have shown is clearly genuine and you are fully aware of the impact your actions have had on your mother and her life. You have to live with the harm you have done, and that will not be easy.'

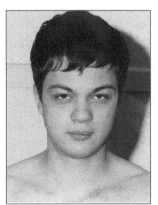

He then sentenced Andrejs to five years imprisonment, but because he had already spent nearly seven months in custody, he would be liable for release within two years. He was, in fact, released in 2009.

Andrejs Hohlovs. (*Hampshire Constabulary History Society*)

2007 – NEIL HAMPSON – A LOVABLE ROGUE

Neil William Hampson, 32, a local builder of Magnolia Road, Merry Oak, was said by his friends and family, who knew him by his nickname of 'Bones', to be a lovable rogue who lived life to the full and made people laugh. This was brought to an abrupt end on the evening of Friday 2 November 2007, when he attended a party in Isla Jarvis's flat on the 12th floor of Havre Towers, International Way, Weston.

The party was celebrating Danielle Gibbon's 21st birthday and the flat was packed with about 20 of her friends, including Isla Jarvis's boyfriend, Tony Wilkinson, 28, who lived in Merrow Avenue, Poole. Wilkinson was wanted by the police in Bournemouth for failing to surrender to his bail after being convicted of attacking a man with a mace, slashing another with a Stanley knife, burglary and theft.

Just before 2am the following morning Wilkinson started to quarrel with Neil William Hampson. Both had been smoking crack cocaine in the kitchen and the initial cause of the disagreement is unknown, but it resulted in the two men fighting furiously in the hallway.

The flat was packed with partygoers and in the confusion, as the two men fought, others screamed in panic when they heard the noise of glass smashing and the two men shouting at each other. Wilkinson was seen to pull a large curved machete-type knife, around 12 inches long, from his waist and strike rapid blows, in quick succession, into Hampson's body and throat. The two men were then pulled apart by several of the guests.

Rebecca Ferguson, one of the guests, saw Wilkinson brandishing a knife and shouting, 'I'll kill you', before being pushed out of the door by his girlfriend, Isla Jarvis. Hampson, covered in blood and looking dazed, was holding his T-shirt away from his

body, revealing a large gash. He said to Rebecca, 'Look what he has done to me' and then slowly slid down the wall onto the floor, unconscious.

Another partygoer who was present, Emma Sullivan, a nurse, saw there was blood everywhere, on the wall, on the floor and on Hampson's clothes. His left ear was cut clean in half and he was bleeding from several places on his body. He then stopped breathing and went blue so, helped by Rebecca Ferguson, she gave him CPR and he started to breathe again.

Havre Towers, Weston (undergoing refurbishment in 2012).

The partygoers left the flat as an ambulance was called and when it arrived Hampson was taken to the Southampton General Hospital. In spite of intensive medical attention he died there an hour and a half later from multiple stab wounds. A subsequent post-mortem revealed he had been stabbed more than 20 times, including in the throat. Stab wounds in the chest had penetrated his heart, lung and kidney.

Earlier, before the ambulance and the police arrived, two men, Daniel Fowler and Lloyd Besnard, were walking in nearby Seaweed Close, towards International Way, when Wilkinson approached them. He had a shaven head, with blood running down his face, and aggressively demanded to know what they were looking at. He then reached down his top and pulled out a large curved knife, threatening them, so they both ran away in different directions. Wilkinson then went across to nearby Barnfield Road, where he stole a 4x4 car and drove away.

A major operation, with the code name Operation Whycliffe, started on the arrival of the police, with the identity of the attacker immediately coming to light and Wilkinson's photograph and description was circulated to surrounding forces. The stolen 4x4 vehicle was found in Throop Mill car park, on the outskirts of Bournemouth, where an attempt had been made to set it alight, and all addresses known to be used by Wilkinson were searched. He was finally traced to a flat owned by Amanda Reeves, his former girlfriend, and arrested by Dorset officers at 5pm that day. He was said to have taken a cocktail of cannabis, crack cocaine and benzodiazepine before his arrest. When taken to Southampton police headquarters for interview he declined to answer questions, other than to say 'no comment'.

Amanda Reeves was also arrested as it was discovered she had collected Wilkinson from her sister's home in Dorset and taken him to her own flat. He had told her he was beaten up by a group of black men but didn't want to talk about it. She later discovered he was wanted by the police after being told it had been on the news. She then took a bag of bloodstained clothes Wilkinson had given her, splashed petrol on them and burnt them on a bonfire. Miss Reeves also dumped a bag of more than 20 knives, owned by Wilkinson, in

a wood near her home. When she was interviewed she said that Wilkinson had a fascination with knives, keeping the bag of more than 20 of them in her flat and often pretended to be 'Rambo', a film character. The knife used to stab Hampson was never found by the police, although giant recycling bins around Havre Towers, nearby Mayfield Park and woodlands in the Throop Mill area were all meticulously searched.

Tony Wilkinson. (*Courtesy of Hampshire Constabulary*)

Wilkinson was charged with the murder of Neil Hampson, producing a blade in public and arson, and appeared before Judge Peter Rook QC at Winchester Crown Court on 1 July 2009. In the course of the three-week trial witnesses who were at the birthday party gave evidence of seeing the stabbing and its aftermath, but Wilkinson persisted in denying being responsible. He also stated that his solicitors had advised him not to speak to officers after his arrest, denying an allegation by the prosecuting counsel, Oba Nsugbe QC that he had waited to see what evidence the police had before he made up a story that would fit.

When giving evidence on his own behalf he said Hampson had mocked him when they were taking drugs in the kitchen, saying, 'I will punch your head in', but Wilkinson had not taken this seriously. He then walked to the toilet, where he smoked some crack cocaine, and then heard a fight starting outside.

He said, 'I heard banging against the walls and the sound of glass breaking, and when I went out 'Bones' stumbled against me and turned his aggression onto me. He started punching me and I punched him back. I was aware of blood when he was on top of me, it was on my face and all over me.'

Wilkinson told the jury that someone pulled Hampson away from him before he fell into the bedroom and grabbed two Gurkha-style knives he had previously hidden there. He denied having used them on Hampson, saying he then ran out of the flat, but admitting he had threatened the two men outside. He added, 'I don't know for certain who stabbed him'.

On Wednesday 29 July 2009 at the conclusion of the four-week trial, the jury took more than 15 hours to deliver a verdict of guilty on all counts. The judge told Wilkinson, 'You're a man who's obsessed with knives and who will erupt into violence.' He then sentenced him to life imprisonment,

to serve a minimum of 17 and a half years, with further sentences of three years for producing a blade in public, two for burglary, two for theft and two for arson, all to be served concurrently with his life sentence.

Neil is buried in St Mary's Extra Cemetery, in plot H47-168, with his father, William Walter Hampson, who died in 1997, and the headstone reads:

NEIL WILLIAM HAMPSON, 'BONES'
IN MEMORY OF A BELOVED SON, BROTHER,
FATHER & PARTNER AND DEEPLY MISSED BY
ALL HIS MUCKERS.
THE BEST PART OF ME WAS ALWAYS YOU. LOVE
AND MISS YOU ALWAYS. LOU LOU
1974 - 2007

The entrance of Havre Towers, where another murder had taken place, that of Paul Berry, who was kicked to death in August 1996. (See *Southampton's Murder Victims*)

Neil William Hampson (as depicted on his headstone).

2007 – LEWIS JAKE SINGLETON – 'THE WRONG PLACE AT THE WRONG TIME'

Lewis Jake Singleton was a decent young man, the third of four children, who grew up in the St Mary's district before the family moved to Upper Weston Lane, Newtown, on the opposite side of the River Itchen. In 2005 at the age of 16, after leaving Woolston Secondary School he worked at Southampton Football Club, first as a catering assistant, then as a barman.

He was a most enthusiastic 'Saints' supporter and described by the deputy manager of Saints Hospitality as 'a very loyal and likeable member of our matchday staff'. He had also played football for his school, scoring 11 goals in 19 games. This was said by the team manager to be 'a pretty good record by a loveable, likeable guy, cheeky faced and never causing harm to anyone'.

By 2007 Lewis had also developed a great interest in music, writing his own songs under the nickname 'Ruffian'. One of his friends later said about him, 'He was always smiling and could make people laugh with his cheeky grin. He was very loving and caring.'

This, then, was the 18-year-old teenager who, on the evening of Saturday 31 March 2007, went out with a group of friends, including an acquaintance he had met a month ago, Craig Smith, 19, to the Grove Tavern, Swift Road, to enjoy a drum and bass night.

They later joined other friends in Yates, Above Bar, before leaving them to walk home together across the Itchen Bridge and along John's Road towards Obelisk Road at around 2am.

Lewis Singleton, enjoying his favourite interest. (*Jenny Singleton*)

Unbeknown to them, five other young men were cruising around Thornhill, Sholing and Woolston in a silver Vauxhall Vectra car, looking for trouble. Two of them were Rikki Johnson, 18, a roofer of Honeysuckle Road, Bassett and Sercan Calik, 18, of Burgess Road, Bassett.

Johnson had been arrested 25 times and had 12 previous convictions, including two for battery, another for intimidating a witness with intent to obstruct or interfere with justice, and one, in 2006, for punching a police officer, for which he received four months in a detention centre.

The one-way John's Road, at its junction with Obelisk Road.

He had only been released six weeks earlier, when he committed a burglary, for which he was electronically tagged. He had also drunk five litre-bottles of alcopops during the course of the night. The three others in the car were youths under the age of 18.

As the Vectra drove over the Itchen Bridge Johnson saw Lewis and Craig leave the bridge and walk into John's Road, a one-way road. He said, 'I've got a problem with that boy; I'm going to beat him up.'

The car was then driven at a very fast speed past the two teenagers, the wrong way along John's Road, into Obelisk Road, where they stopped.

As the couple reached them Johnson jumped out of the car with one of the others, and, without warning, ran aggressively across to the two youngsters. Craig immediately ran away but Lewis was caught up by Johnson, who was then joined by his four friends. He said, 'What's up?' and was then, without warning, attacked by the group.

Craig, who had run the length of Obelisk Road, towards Victoria Road, looked back and saw that all five had surrounded Lewis, who had fallen to the ground opposite John's Road, being kicked as he lay there.

Lewis was heard pleading with his attackers, 'Leave me alone now, you've done me, you've done me!' He then managed to stagger up and break away from the group surrounding him, running towards Craig Smith. As he passed him he cried out, 'I've been stabbed, I've been stabbed' and continued running to the bottom of Obelisk Road, across Victoria Road into Condor Close, where he collapsed.

The gang of five had by then returned to the Vectra and drove down to Victoria Road, looking for Craig, seeing Lewis fall to the ground in Condor Close as they did so. They then drove off, Johnson boasting that he had 'done a proper job' on Lewis.

Craig then went to Lewis, saw he had a wound in his stomach and phoned from his nearby home for an ambulance, which arrived shortly afterwards and took Lewis to the General Hospital. It was found that he had sustained five stab wounds but despite all the doctors' efforts, and blood transfusions, he died eight hours later. He had also

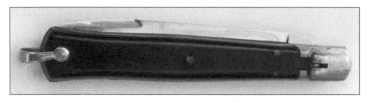

A 10cm bladed flick knife, similar to the one found at Calik's home.

sustained a fatal head wound as a result of being kicked in the head as he lay on the ground. The incident had now become a murder investigation and was given the code name Operation Keane.

Police had been quickly on the scene and, on being told the registered number of the Vectra, traced Sercan Calik, the owner, to his flat above a kebab shop in Burgess Road. Calik was arrested and a subsequent search traced a flick knife hidden in a petrol can in the yard outside his home.

A subsequent post-mortem revealed that Lewis had been stabbed right through his right arm, with further stabbings puncturing his left lung, diaphragm and liver. The latter three alone were so severe that each could have been fatal, but the stabbing that finally killed the unfortunate Lewis was one in his abdomen that severed the major artery to his right leg.

As a result of questioning Calik, plus further enquiries, the remaining four occupants of the Vectra, including Johnson, were quickly traced and arrested. Two of them were only aged 15 and one was 16. Interviewed over several days they all gave different accounts as to what had happened.

One explanation for the attack, given by Johnson, was that earlier that evening he and a friend had been chased by someone carrying a knife. He had therefore phoned Sercan Calik to pick him and the others up in his Vectra car to go looking for the youth who had chased him with a knife.

Calik had brought his flick knife with him and passed it over to Johnson. When they saw Craig and Lewis together Johnson thought he recognised Craig as the one who had chased him, hence the attack. This, however, was shown to be completely untrue, it was a either a case of mistaken identity or a mere excuse to be violent. Johnson agreed he possessed the flick knife, and had used it, but said it was to protect his friends. He said he was trying to stab his arm but missed it and hit the stomach.

When later asked if he had tried to cut Lewis he said 'Yeah, stick it in. After the first one he didn't even feel it go in and didn't see no blood about it. I'm not going to say I didn't use a lot of force because I was worried about my mate. After the first one he didn't even back away and then I done it again. Because I could see he wasn't letting go I thought the knife didn't even go in. Everyone was still hitting him because no one realised he was hurt.'

Top: Rikki Johnson (*Courtesy of Hampshire Constabulary*) and bottom Sercan Calik. (*Hampshire Constabulary History Society*)

Calik denied owning the flick knife, but others in the gang said they saw him passing it to Johnson, who added that everyone knew it belonged to Calik.

Four of the five were later charged with murder, manslaughter and violent disorder, with the remaining youngster released without charge. Although this youth was thought to be the original main attacker with Johnson, there was insufficient evidence for him to be brought before the court. The four were all subsequently committed to Winchester Crown Court, where they appeared before Mr Justice David Steel on 21 January 2008 and pleaded 'not guilty'.

Evidence was given of the statements made by the accused when in custody but Calik continued to deny he had ever owned the flick knife. He said it belonged to Johnson and that he was not involved in the death of Lewis at all.

There was much conflicting evidence given in the course of the trial, that continued well over three weeks, but there was little doubt that, in fact, the knife had been originally produced by Calik. Johnson also told the court, 'When I saw Lewis Singleton go to his pocket I tried to stop him by stabbing him in his right arm. But I think it slipped off his arm and went towards his stomach. Lewis carried on fighting so I tried stabbing him in the backside to stop him.'

Medical reports did not reveal any evidence of hand injuries to Lewis and it was clear that he, in fact, had no real opportunity to fight back while being hit by five men simultaneously.

On 15 February at the conclusion of the trial, Johnson was unanimously found guilty of murder and violent disorder and sentenced to life imprisonment, to serve a minimum of 15 years. It was then revealed that he was subject to a night-time curfew, wearing an electronic tag, but had repeatedly broken the order by leaving his home between 9pm and 7am as well as breaking the conditions by turning up late to his unpaid work sessions.

Calik was convicted of manslaughter and sentenced to eight years. Of the remaining two juveniles, one, a 16-year-old, was acquitted when the jury failed to reach a unanimous verdict.

The other, also unnamed throughout the trial for legal reasons, was acquitted of murder and manslaughter after the jury retired for nearly 22 hours, but convicted of violent disorder. He was then sentenced to two years imprisonment and, for the first time, publicly named. (Although known to the author, he cannot now be named because of the Rehabilitation of Offenders Act.)

Immediately after the murder there was strong public feeling of sympathy for Lewis' family and an enormous amount of affection shown for the victim of the unprovoked attack. A huge amount of flowers were placed at the scene of the attack, with messages left by his large number of friends. The local newspaper the *Southern Daily Echo* also

The site of the attack in Obelisk Road. The photograph was taken in early December 2011 but the flowers were fresh.

The lovingly made mosaic plaque is mounted on the wall as a permanent shrine in memory of an innocent young man.

mounted a campaign, 'Carrying a Blade, It's Not Sharp', to keep knives off the street and friends and family of Lewis had T-shirts made, bearing the teenager's picture, to highlight the cost of carrying knives. Although the unfortunate Lewis was cremated, the permanent memorial soon came into being in Obelisk Road.

Lewis' mother, Jeanette Singleton, now works for the national charity 'Through UNITY', helping the families of other victims and later campaigned against an EU proposal to give prisoners the right to vote.

She also said, 'People say my son was in the wrong place at the wrong time. He was in the right place at the right time. It was the killers who were in the wrong place at the wrong time.'

2008 – ELLIE & ISOBELLE CASS – 'THEY ARE ASLEEP FOREVER'

These were the frightening words heard by Kerry Hughes at 6.45pm on Sunday 21 September 2008, when her partner, David Cass, 33, a car mechanic, phoned her. The couple had parted, acrimoniously, four months earlier and he was living in a caravan parked at the rear of a garage in Paynes Road, Shirley. He had worked there as a self-employed MoT tester for the previous four years.

The couple had two children, Ellie Marie Cass, aged three and Isobelle Frances Cass, aged 14 months, and David was looking after them that weekend. When he phoned her he said 'They are asleep'. She asked him what he meant and he replied, 'They are asleep forever and I'm going to hang myself. Just remember, I will always love you.'

He had already told her, on the previous Friday evening, that he was going to take his own life, but she hadn't believed him. It was not the first time he had threatened suicide but it had always turned out to be just a cry for attention. He had never suggested in any way that he would also harm the children.

But as a result of the phone call, which sounded so ominous, Kerry became somewhat hysterical and phoned the police, who immediately went to the garage and car sales in Paynes Road. Two ambulances and three rapid response paramedic vehicles also attended the scene.

The car sales forecourt was enclosed with high level fencing and the police had to force a locked gate off its hinges to gain entry to the premises. David Cass' caravan was parked at the rear of the site and when officers entered it they saw the two children lying side by side on a bunk.

The girls were clearly dead and an immediate search was made for David Cass. It was now a murder investigation, given the code name Operation Roselands.

The murder scene caravan. (*Hampshire Constabulary History Society*)

Right: Another view of the caravan, showing the open garage door where Cass was found. Left: An inside view of part of the caravan. (*Hampshire Constabulary History Society*)

He was soon found, hanging by the neck with rope from a beam in the adjacent garage building, also obviously dead. His mobile phone was found on the ground underneath him, with a step ladder lying on its side, indicating it had been kicked away when he stood on it with a rope around his neck. It became clear that he had committed suicide directly after phoning the girls' mother.

Subsequent post-mortems showed the girls had been smothered and their father had died by strangulation. The funeral of the two toddlers took place on 10 October at the Eastleigh Holy Cross Roman Catholic Church, when more than 100 mourners packed the church.

Inside the garage, showing the overturned step ladder. (*Hampshire Constabulary History Society*)

The official plan produced at court, showing the site of the murder and suicide.

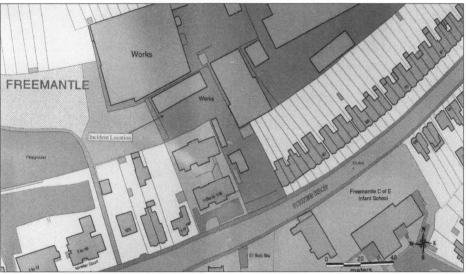

The site today, with the gates open and garage in the background.

The two girls are buried in the Ramally Cemetery, Chandlers Ford, side by side in graves b.22 and b.23.

At an inquest held on 27 November 2008 Det.Sgt Glyn White told the jury that on the day of the deaths Cass had called old friends he had not spoken to for years. He had also called his mother, Lynn Cass, to say he could not let the children return to live with their mother. It had been the first time he had looked after the children on his own. He then said to his mother, before hanging up, 'The children have gone to sleep and so am I. I love you Mum.'

The verdict at the inquest was that of unlawful death for the two girls and of suicide for David Cass.

2008 – HOLLIE GREEN – 'THE LOVE OF YOUR LIFE'

Hollie Jane Green, 21, an optician employed by the local Specsavers, had obtained a diploma at Kent University, where she qualified as a dispensing optician and had also undertaken a management course to become a locum optician, travelling around the south. She was a talented sportswoman, a former member of the Solent Stars basketball team and a member of a local amateur dramatic club.

The block of flats in Taranto Road.

At about 4.15am on Sunday 31 August 2008, after a 'girlie night out' and accompanied by her friends, Hollie returned to her third-floor flat in a block of 12 in Taranto Road, overlooking Lord's Hill Way, Lordswood.

Daniel Lee Gibbens, 21, a carpenter and partner from whom she was separated, suddenly arrived on the scene and bundled her into the flat, leaving her friends outside. They then heard him bolt the door from the inside, followed by the sound of Hollie screaming for help.

Inside Hollie Green's flat. (*Hampshire Constabulary History Society*)

Their repeated knocking failed to get a response, although the screaming continued. The screaming then stopped abruptly and further knocking was met with complete silence. Daniel Gibbens then shouted at them, telling them to leave them alone. Alarmed by the continued silence, the police were called, and on their arrival a decision was taken to break down the door to gain entry.

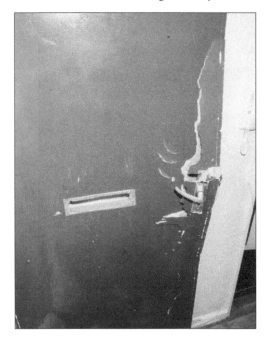

The flat door, after the forced entry. (*Hampshire Constabulary History Society*)

Inside, on the bedroom floor, they found the clearly dead body of Hollie Green, as well as the apparently unconscious body of Daniel Gibbens, who was taken to the General Hospital by ambulance. A murder investigation team was formed immediately, with the codename Operation Barnaby.

Hollie showed signs of strangulation, and when Gibbens was later discharged from the hospital, with no evidence of injury or explanation for his apparent unconsciousness, he was taken to Shirley police station for questioning.

He was then told that Hollie was dead, a medical examination confirming she had been strangled, and he admitted that he had forcibly placed both his hands around her neck, while looking away from her, after she had thrown a couple of punches at him when they argued in the bedroom over whether or not he could return to the flat. He added he had taken a small amount of cocaine just before her death, together with some alcohol.

After declining the offer of legal advice, he further explained the background of their relationship.

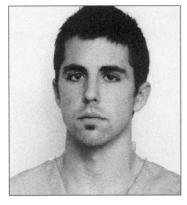

Daniel Lee Gibbens. (*Hampshire Constabulary History Society*)

The two had met at Oaklands School when they were very young, and after leaving school their relationship deepened. They initially set up home with Hollie's parents, but then moved into their own flat in Taranto Road, followed by the birth of their daughter in 2005.

Hollie subsequently accused him of cheating on her with another girl, something he denied, but he agreed to move out of the flat while they resolved the issue. Hollie then began to believe him and he stayed over at the flat a few times and it was agreed he would later move back permanently. However, pictures were later posted on an internet social networking site showing him kissing another girl, and this considerably upset Hollie.

She also discovered that he had sent a 'Happy Valentine's Day' text to another woman in response to one he had received. Daniel said Hollie had then given him mixed messages, sending him a birthday card for his 21st birthday in August, which she signed 'All my love', but becoming hostile when she saw him while with her friends.

Gibbens was charged with her murder, appeared before Judge Guy Boney QC in June 2009 and pleaded 'not guilty' to the charge but admitted manslaughter. Giving evidence on his own behalf he told the court, 'When you wake up and you are coming round and somebody tells you that the love of your life is dead and it is because of you, it is the worst feeling in the world. All I wanted to do was just die there and then.'

Contrary to what he told the police after his arrest, he told the court that Hollie had thrown a lot of punches at him, which is why he had to restrain her. He had also taken far more cocaine and alcohol than he initially said but could not explain the medical evidence that showed only small traces in his system. He now said that he had not placed two hands around her throat but only used one hand on her neck to fend her off when she attacked him.

After deliberating for five hours the jury of three women and nine men returned a verdict of guilty of murder. Judge Boney said it was clear that Gibbens had gone round to the flat in the early hours to confront Hollie after she had sent him a text telling him to leave her alone and describing him as 'a loser'. He said, 'You brooded on it and you went round there to have it out with her. You seized her by the throat and over the next few minutes you took her life.'

He then sentenced Gibbens to life, to spend at least 13 years before being considered for parole.

Hollie Green is buried in Hollybrook Cemetery, in plot K21-57 and the headstone reads:

HOLLIE JANE GREEN LOVING
DAUGHTER, MUM & SISTER
SUNRISE 18.12.1986
SUNSET 31.08.2008
FOREVER IN OUR HEARTS, YOU WILL
ALWAYS STAY
UNTIL WE MEET AGAIN ONE DAY.

Hollie Jane Green, as depicted on her headstone.

2008 – EMMA AMY – AN INTERNET RELATIONSHIP

Emma Amy, 26, had been married for nine years to Gavin Amy, 30, with whom she had three children, aged nine, seven and four. However, the marriage had broken down by Christmas 2007, when she asked him for a divorce.

Gavin took this badly and on Thursday 10 January 2008, seriously assaulted Emma during an argument. The following day he tried to commit suicide, while the children were at home, and was found unconscious by his wife. Following his admission to the General Hospital he became a voluntary psychiatric patient, telling the consultant psychiatrist that he considered killing his wife by strangulation and then killing himself.

He said he planned to do this in front of his children, but at the end of six days of treatment said he no longer had thoughts of killing her and now accepted the fact that they would be divorced. The doctors were satisfied that his stay had helped him to recover. He then discharged himself, against medical advice, and returned to their third floor council flat in Wimpson Lane.

The flat, at the far right, at the end of the corridor, in the Wimpson Lane block.

Three days later, on Thursday 17 January 2008, he logged onto his wife's email account and discovered she had been having an internet relationship with a man she had met online. He read that the couple were due to spend a night together in a London hotel. This enraged him and he confronted her about it, in front of the children, demanding to know the man's name and more about the relationship. He then lost control and grasped her throat, preventing her from breathing. His eldest son tried to stop him but the children were ordered out of the room.

Neighbours in the corridor heard screaming and gathered outside the door, trying to force an entry, but the screaming stopped suddenly. They rang the police, who arrived soon afterwards. By then Gavin had phoned his parents, asking them to come and collect the children.

When the police, followed by paramedics, entered the flat they found Emma dead on the floor with the children hysterical and the youngest child vomiting. When they tried to resuscitate their mother Gavin said, 'There's no point doing that, she's been like that for a while.' Mrs Amy was pronounced dead at the scene and a murder investigation was started under the code name Operation Radley. Amy's husband was subsequently arrested for her murder and a post-mortem confirmed she had been strangled.

He appeared before Mr Justice Royce at the Winchester Crown Court on Tuesday 10 March 2009, and pleaded 'guilty'. The judge told him that the killing would be a haunting memory for certainly two of the children and sentenced him to life imprisonment, to serve a minimum of 15 years, less two and a half years for his guilty plea, making a total of 12 years and six months.

Gavin Amy. (*Courtsey of Hampshire Constabulary*)

2009 – MARGARET KIBUUKA – 'A COLD AND CALCULATING KILLING'

On 9 November 2010 Mr Justice Royce addressed George Kibuuka, 47, in the dock at Winchester Crown Court. Jailing him for life, to serve a minimum of 16 years, he told him 'You are a controlling man who carried out a savage killing that will haunt your children for the rest of their lives. This was a terrible savage killing of an intelligent, gentle and loving mother. It was a selfish, cold and calculating killing.'

George Kibuuka had met young teenage Margaret Nanozi in the late 1980s in Uganda, where they had an initial local marriage ceremony, but he fled the country's violence in the early 1990s and came to England to start a new life. As a teenager he had obtained a scholarship to Macquarie University, Kampala, where he studied statistics and obtained a good degree, Master of Science. There was no question that he was a clever student.

Margaret joined him later and they bought their home in Richville Road, Shirley, where they became the proud parents of three young boys and a girl.

The Kibuuka family home in Richville Road. (*Hampshire Constabulary History Society*)

By the end of the century he had become a wealthy IT consultant, earning £90,000 a year with a pharmaceutical company, and had purchased four properties in the Southampton area as well as substantial land in his native Uganda. In 2000 they briefly returned to Uganda where they re-married in Kampala, celebrating with family and friends in the luxury Sheraton Hotel.

However, all was not well underneath the veneer of luxury and wealth. By the summer of 2002 he had become abusive and once badly beat and punched her in the face during an argument, pushing her violently down the stairs. Margaret was then attending Southampton Solent University taking a business and economics course and had to remain at home for some time because of her swollen face and eye.

She later believed that her husband had been having an affair with her sister, as well as other affairs, so in August 2009, at the age of 39 and after 22 years of living with George, decided to start divorce proceedings. George was very angry about this as he did not want the prospect of his wealth being shared with her. As the violence continued she went to Shirley police station on 24 August, saying she was worried about his irrational behaviour. Although she had started divorce proceedings, they remained living in the same house, but sleeping in separate rooms. Margaret was later taken to a police specialist video suite where she described various incidents, including a statement that, 'Anything could happen at any time, he's unpredictable. One of these days something is going to happen.'

Her prediction came true just over two months later, on Saturday 7 November, when George made a calculated and gruesome decision. He went to the West Quay and Tesco pharmacies, with three of his children, and purchased sedatives comprising 50 Sleepezee tablets and two packets of paracetamol.

Further CCTV footage, showed them entering Tesco Express, and receipts found in the house revealed he had bought a Christmas Yule Log, two packets of paracetamol and a chef's knife for £18.

CCTV showing them entering Tesco Express. (*Hampshire Constabulary History Society*)

On his return home he crushed and dissolved 10 50mg tablets into bottles of Coke and Fanta and into a trifle, which he gave to the children that evening. He later said that he did this so they would be unaware of what he was about to do.

The family then watched a film and the children went to bed, leaving their mother downstairs studying on her personal computer for her business course. Both parents later went to bed in their respective rooms, but at around 4.30am George got up and logged onto his wife's PC.

He had secretly installed surveillance equipment on it, monitoring the sites she had visited and her email accounts. He found that she had typed several questions into a search engine, such things as 'Will I ever get over the break up of my marriage?', 'Why can't my ex-husband move on and leave me alone?' and 'My ex won't leave the house'.

He then took a heavy sledgehammer that he had secreted in his bedroom drawer and went to the adjoining bedroom, where his wife was sleeping with their young daughter in a drugged state beside her. Without turning on the light he smashed his sleeping wife on the head with two massive blows of the hammer.

He then switched on the light and, as he said later, 'to minimise the pain', took the kitchen knife and cut her throat, so deep as to reach his wife's spine. (Home Office pathologist Dr Hugh White later told the court that Margaret had sustained a fractured skull, with a 2cm laceration above her right ear, and her windpipe, thyroid gland and left jugular vein had all been severed in the attack.)

George then carried his sleeping daughter into his bedroom before covering his wife's body with the bedcovers. Going downstairs he poured a bottle of insecticide into a glass of water and drank it.

After phoning his sister and asking her to come to Southampton and look after his children, he went upstairs, took the knife he had used to cut his wife's throat, pushed it into his stomach and laid on his bed, covering himself with a blanket.

Later that Sunday morning the eldest son woke up when he heard his younger brother and sister screaming and crying. He went into his mother's bedroom and saw his dead mother on the bed with a massive amount of blood running down from her neck onto the floor. Going into his father's room he again saw a lot of blood and was unable to wake his father, who was apparently dead.

The upper landing and bedroom doors.
(*Hampshire Constabulary History Society*)

The children ran out into the street and knocked on the door of a neighbour, Mrs Muriel Westerman, telling her that somebody had killed their parents. The police were called and when they arrived PC Charman went to the middle bedroom where he found Margaret's body. He then remained at the entrance of the bedroom to preserve the scene.

PC Taylor then went to the front bedroom where he found George wrapped from head to foot in bloodstained bedding. When he removed the bedding he saw what appeared to be a stab wound in the chest and that he was apparently dead. A large metal knife, with both the handle and blade bloodstained, was next to George's right hand side.

The heavily bloodstained hammer, weighing 6.5kg, and knife with a 20cm blade, used to kill Margaret Kibuuka. (*Hampshire Constabulary History Society*)

Bloodstains on the bedroom floor, with special trays that avoid contamination and enable officers to walk over the floor and carry out further examinations. (*Hampshire Constabulary History Society*)

Shoe impressions in blood on the bedroom floor. (*Hampshire Constabulary History Society*)

Empty bottles of Kayazinon. (*Hampshire Constabulary History Society*)

It then became apparent that George Kibuuka was still alive and he was taken to hospital and placed on a life support machine. It became apparent that he had ingested a hazardous substance as hospital staff started to experience eye irritation and coughing. He was diagnosed as suffering from significant organic phosphate poisoning and remained seriously ill for nearly two weeks. (A search of the front bedroom had revealed five small empty containers of the pesticide 'Kayazinon'.)

He then sufficiently recovered to be interviewed and as a result was arrested on 29 November and charged with his wife's murder and three counts of drugging his children. Toxicology tests on the children's urine had revealed detectable traces of sleeping tablets and diazepam. The tests had also revealed traces of sleeping tablets in the remains of a trifle found in the house and traces of pesticide in a glass jug containing a small amount of liquid.

Kibuuka's mobile phone was checked and the last text message on it was to his sister at 5.50am 8 November, in a Ugandan language, translated as 'Forgive me'.

He appeared at Winchester Crown Court on 18 October 2010, and pleaded 'not guilty' to the charges. During his three-week trial Kibuuka admitted killing his wife but said in evidence that he only intended to break her legs with the hammer 'so she would be dependant on me and

George Kibuuka. (*Courtsey of Hampshire Constabulary*)

have a need for me'. It was only when he switched on the light that he realised his mistake and needed to cut her throat to ease her pain.

The court heard the taped police interview the deceased had made in August 2009, as well as a video of the eldest son's interview with the police the day after the murder. They also heard a series of recorded police interviews with George Kibuuka after his arrest.

Mr Nigel Pascoe QC, defending Kibuuka, argued that he was suffering from an abnormality of mind that substantially diminished his responsibility for his actions, but after retiring for under five hours the jury did not agree. Kibuuka was then sentenced to life imprisonment.

The unfortunate Margaret Kibuuka is buried in plot X104 in Ramally Cemetery, Chandlers Ford, marked with a simple cross stating:

MARGARET KIBUUKA
DIED 8TH NOVEMBER 2009
AGED 40 YEARS.

2009 – NIGEL PRICE – AN UNSOLVED KILLING

Openly gay and chronic alcoholic Nigel Price, 58, of Heather Court, Thornhill, called the police to his home on the evening of Friday 13 November 2009 and when they attended they found he had self-harmed. He became hostile towards the police and was taken to the General Hospital by ambulance, but he discharged himself before being treated.

Nigel then went to where he was well known, the Cowherds public house on Southampton Common and was captured by CCTV leaving the premises at 8.20pm. He was walking towards the Common's nearby Cemetery Road, an area known to be frequented by gay people at night.

A passer-by called the police 20 minutes later, at 8.40pm, saying he thought a possible homophobic attack was taking place after he saw two men approach a man and then hear loud shouting. An hour later two other persons dialled '999' after they found a man covered in blood and staggering around on the Common, but who refused help. In neither case were the police able to take any effective action.

At 7.30am the following morning a dog walker found Nigel Price semi-conscious, partially clothed and face down in bushes on the Common. Paramedics were called, found he was suffering from serious head injuries and he was taken to the General Hospital. He was able to give them his name and details before his condition seriously deteriorated and he slipped into a coma.

Nigel Price. (*Hampshire Constabulary History Society*)

Detectives made extensive enquiries, with the area closely examined by Scenes of Crime officers, and appeals were made in the media for information, all without any real success. Interviews were also carried out with regular users of the Common, but detectives were met with a wall of silence.

Despite intensive medical care Nigel Price remained in a coma until he finally died on 23 March 2010, after fighting for his life for over four months. The consequent murder investigation, with the code name Operation Levy, was intensified, without any significant progress, and on the first anniversary of his death, a £10,000 reward was offered for information leading to a conviction. This was funded by donations from Hampshire Constabulary and the charity 'Crimestoppers Trust'.

A post-mortem showed Nigel had been repeatedly kicked or struck on the head with a heavy blunt instrument and despite continuous efforts to reduce the consequent swelling of his brain, he was judged too weak to survive lengthy high-risk surgery. When he died 5ft 6in Nigel weighed just six and a half stone. He was subsequently cremated.

His older brother, Tony Price, who travelled from his home in Wales, said, 'Seeing the photographs of his injuries I just couldn't believe what had happened to him. He didn't deserve this, he didn't deserve to die.'

At the adjourned inquest, held on 7 March 2011, HM Coroner, Mr Keith Wiseman, recorded a verdict of 'unlawful killing'.

Any reader who has useful information should call Hampshire Constabulary on 101, or 'Crimestoppers' anonymously, on 0800 555 111, quoting 'Operation Levy'.

2010 – MARIA SZARVAK – AN 'OPEN MARRIAGE' THAT FAILED

Maria Szarvak, 37, and her husband, Sandor Lakatos, 38, had enjoyed the modern phenomenon, an 'open marriage', until it went wrong. They had come to England from Hungary in the summer of 2008, renting a house in Harcourt Road, Bitterne. The couple had met when both were studying at a Hungarian university and after being together for eight years they finally married in 2000. Both were fully qualified pharmacists, working at Boots, but Sandor was under some strain because of a heavy workload, together with the numerous affairs enjoyed by his wife which made him feel inadequate.

It wasn't until late 2008 that the open marriage had been agreed. He had experienced a 'one night stand' while on a course and she had enjoyed a sexual relationship with two other men. When she asked him for an open marriage so she could see other men, he had felt rather humiliated about it. However, he agreed and they then both had other lovers, meeting them through an internet dating site.

Arguments started soon after their arrival in England, primarily because Sandor was spending too much time at work, and the position deteriorated to the point where in late 2009 they had separate beds. In November that year he left to live in Portsmouth and they spoke of returning to Hungary to get divorced, but the situation improved somewhat and he began to regularly visit their marital home.

On the morning of Wednesday 7 July 2010, Maria did her usual shopping at Tesco while Sandor did the ironing. They had earlier agreed to go to Gunwharf Quays, Portsmouth, together but on her return an argument broke out when she refused to go to Portsmouth and told him to leave the house. What Sandor did not know was that she had already agreed to meet one of her internet lovers, Colin Calverley, later that day. The two regularly had sex at her home in Harcourt Road.

The argument became violent, in the course of which Maria was

The scene of the murder in Harcourt Road.

thrown through a rear door glass pane. Sandor then grabbed a kitchen knife, stabbing her nine times in her back and chest while they were in the kitchen. She fell to the floor, bleeding heavily, with the knife still protruding from her chest.

He then phoned '999' from the house, telling the operator, 'I have stabbed my wife, she's in the kitchen', before hanging up and rushing from the house.

The police arrived at the scene within minutes and had to break into the locked house, immediately finding Maria lying on her back on the kitchen floor with a large black-handled knife sticking out of her chest. She was barely alive, bleeding heavily, and in spite of officers and paramedics trying to revive her for over 30 minutes, she died at the scene.

Immediate enquiries were made to trace Sandor but this was resolved later that day when a '999' call was made by taxi driver Nicholas Stone from Hordle Cliff, near Milford on Sea. He had found Sandor in a dazed condition in a public toilet, clad only in his underpants and soaking wet, muttering, 'What have I done? What have I done?' Sandor was arrested at a nearby ice cream kiosk and said, 'How is my wife, did she die?' He said he had tried to drown himself at Beckton Bunny Beach near Barton-on-Sea golf course. He had driven there, waded into the sea but then changed his mind, driving to Hordle Cliff to give himself up.

He was taken to Southampton, where he made a statement under caution admitting having stabbed his wife, in which he said, 'I recall blocking my wife's path, stopping her from leaving the kitchen and remember stabbing her once in the back and once in the chest'.

He was charged with the murder and appeared before Judge Guy Boney QC, and a five-man and seven-woman jury at Hampshire Crown Court, Winchester, on Monday 13 June 2011.

In the course of the trial Alastair Macolm QC, prosecuting, said the key question was whether Sandor was suffering from diminished responsibility or could claim

provocation. Medical evidence, however, was given that although his suicide attempt was probably genuine, he was not suffering from any mental disorder.

Sandor gave evidence, saying 'a red fog had descended on me'. He agreed he had stabbed her but didn't remember holding the knife in his hand. He only remembered stabbing her once in the back and once in the chest and was unable to explain why he had done it.

Sandor Lakatos. (*Hampshire Constabulary History Society*)

Richard Fry, a consultant psychiatrist for the defence, said Sandor had lost control because he was faced with the loss of everything he had worked for for the last 23 years. He added that Sandor had been overwhelmed by emotion in such a way that he seems unlikely to have had the capacity to premeditate or deliberately form the intention to kill.

At the conclusion of the trial, that had lasted for 15 days, the jury cleared Sandor of murder but found him guilty of manslaughter due to diminished responsibility. The judge told Sandor, 'Most of the stab wounds your wife received would have been sufficient to kill her. Although your responsibility for the killing was substantially impaired by your state of mind, I take the view that your responsibility isn't by any means minimal. You will go to prison for six and a half years, with the year you have spent in custody being deducted.'

2011 – ANITA BAWTREE – 'YOU'RE A NAZI'

Anita Bawtree, 34, who had mental health issues, was described by one of her neighbours in Napier House, Paynes Road, as 'a really nice quiet lady' and by another as 'polite and well-mannered'.

Anita's partner, Steven Waters, 54, also had mental health problems, but of a far more serious nature. He had fought both alcohol and drug addictions for more than 30 years

The Napier House apartments in Paynes Road, Shirley.

and had been an in-patient at the Department of Psychiatry, Royal South Hants Hospital.

His condition worsened on the evening of 19 April 2011, when he threatened one of their neighbours, pregnant Amy Brady, saying she was stealing his electricity to grow cannabis. She had received a phone call from him threatening to harm her and her child, ordering her to restore his electricity or 'I am coming round'. Because her baby was due within weeks she was frightened and called an ambulance and police, waiting with a paramedic until the police arrived. Waters also made several '999' calls to the police, repeating his allegation, and PC Lance Plummer attended, warning Waters as to his behaviour.

Two hours later, Waters dialled '999' again, this time to say, 'I have killed the only person I have loved'. He called the police again 20 minutes later, but hung up before he could be questioned further about his statement. In view of his earlier unfounded allegations his calls were not taken seriously, but a further call was made around midnight by one of his neighbours saying she had heard shouting and a woman screaming, 'Please, please, please' coming from Waters' flat, before the noise of a thud and then silence. Waters was also heard to scream, 'Somebody help me, my partner's dead'. The police therefore attended immediately, but Waters refused to open the door, repeating that he had killed his partner.

A three-hour siege then started, with specialist negotiating officers and a dog unit attending. When Waters appeared on the flat's balcony, brandishing a knife, throwing items down onto the ground below and setting fire to the curtains, the fire brigade and armed police were called. During the siege Waters was seen slicing his hand with the knife. Eventually, after the fire brigade had hosed down the window curtains and the trained negotiators had failed to persuade him, the door was forced open and Waters overcome by means of a Taser gun.

The officers then found the bloodstained body of Anita Bawtree in the flat, with obvious stab wounds, later found to number 15, to her body, one of them to her heart. Waters was detained and taken to Lyndhurst police station where, in the course of questioning, he said, 'I thought that the whole world was after me, the police, the Government and the Sky News channel. I told her she was a Nazi and that Nazis must die for all the things they've done. She was a Nazi trying to escape. Because she couldn't answer my questions and so forth, I stabbed her, after trying to strangle her. I think the madness got to me so much that I truly believed that she was a Nazi and was going to flee.'

He was charged with the murder and appeared before Judge Keith Cutler at Winchester Crown Court on 24 April 2012, when he pleaded not guilty but admitted manslaughter on the grounds of diminished responsibility. This plea was not accepted by the prosecution and the murder trial continued for the following three weeks.

In the course of the trial Waters gave evidence that, just prior to the murder, he had collided with the wing mirrors of several cars while driving and stopped to speak to the other motorists, telling them that Earth was being attacked by aliens and he would lead them to safety. He admitted killing his partner but said it was because he was under the influence of drugs at the time, making him hallucinate.

However, on 16 May at the conclusion of the trial, the jury, in under an hour, unanimously found him guilty of murder and the judge deferred sentence until the following day. He then told Waters, 'Miss Bawtree was a vulnerable woman recovering from mental illness and you were in a position of trust. You subjected your partner to a most terrifying and violent ordeal. I feel it must have been two hours of mental and physical torture that she was ill-equipped to endure. She died at the hands of a man she loved and to whom she looked for protection.' He then sentenced Waters to life imprisonment, to serve at least 18 years before being considered for parole.

After the verdict Det.Ch.Insp. Chris Fitchit told Warwick Payne, a *Southern Daily Echo* reporter, 'It was a difficult case in the sense that here we had two people who had mental health issues. There was a partial defence of diminished responsibility, which is clearly a difficult area of law for the legal teams and the jury, but we are very satisfied with the verdict. Mr Waters' account was strange, to say the least, and we were fortunate that we had the assistance of eminent experts in this area who were able to help the jury in coming to their verdict. It must be said that this was a tragic case.'

Steven Waters. (*Courtesy of Hampshire Constabulary*)

2011 – IAN MOLYNEUX – AN ACT OF BRAVERY

On Friday 8 April 2011 the submarine HMS *Astute* was berthed in Southampton's Eastern Docks on a goodwill visit, at 97 metres long and weighing 7,400 tonnes, the *Astute* class has the biggest 'ears' of any sonar system in the Royal Navy. It is the Royal Navy's newest submarine and the most sophisticated hunter-killer vessel in the world, guarded by its own crew when in port. Driven by a nuclear reactor, it carries Spearfish torpedoes and Tomahawk cruise missiles.

HMS *Astute* in Southampton Eastern Docks. (*courtesy of Hampshire Constabulary*)

The 98 submariners on board are the first in the Navy to have their own beds; they normally work round the clock and have to share a bunk or bed with someone on the opposite shift pattern, one sleeping while the other is on duty. Their bunks are stacked three high and each submariner has one small locker to store their personal possessions during their three-month tour. However, the captain is the only member to have his own room and wash-hand basin.

Among the crew this day was Lieutenant Commander Ian Molyneux, 36, the vessel's weapons engineering officer, who hailed from Wigan, Lancashire. He was married with four children aged between six and 14.

Also on board was Able Seaman Ryan Samuel Donovan, 23, of Hillside Road, Dartford, Kent, a London-born warfare specialist, trained in tracking vessels. He was in a resentful mood because he had recently been told he would not be attached to the Royal Fleet Auxiliary ship *Cardigan Bay*, as he had requested, because he had disobeyed orders to clean part of the submarine. He was especially upset with Petty Officer Christopher Brown, 36, and Chief Petty Officer David McCoy, 37, about this.

At around noon on Friday 8 April an arranged official visit and tour of the submarine by civic dignitaries took place in Southampton's Eastern Docks. The party included Southampton's Mayor, Carol Cunio, Royston Smith, the council leader and Alistair Neill, the council chief executive.

At the same time AB Ryan Donovan, wearing body armour and camouflage clothing, had just collected his SA80 semi-automatic assault rifle from the weapons store and was about to take up his sentry position on the gangplank, following the changeover between shifts. However, instead of going to his post he went towards the vessel's control room.

As he entered he saw PO Christopher Brown with CPO David McCoy and suddenly, and completely unexpectedly, opened fire from about 10 feet away. He fired four shots, all of which missed their target, but Lt.Cdr Ian Molyneux, hearing the shots, turned round, was immediately shot in the head at close range by Donovan and killed instantly.

Donovan stepped over the body and continued along the control room where he met Lt.Cdr Christopher Hodge, 45, who, without warning, was shot in his stomach and seriously injured.

Before Donovan could continue shooting, Councillor Royston Smith ran towards him, pushed him against the wall as the gun was again fired, and wrestled him to the ground, helped by chief executive Alistair Neill.

Cllr Smith, a former RAF engineer, managed to pull the rifle away and throw it out of Donovan's reach, and the AB was restrained by both officials.

Ryan Donovan's SA80 assault rifle. (*Courtesy of Hampshire Constabulary*)

Investigating Officers on board HMS *Astute*, left to right: Det.Supt Tony Harris; A/Det.Insp. Dave Nealon; Crime Scene Manager Craig Jones and A/Det.Supt Tim Doyle. (*Courtesy of Hampshire Constabulary*)

Cllr Smith suffered bruises to his legs and back, together with a cut to his head, in the struggle, but did not require hospital treatment.

(Lt.Cdr. Christopher Hodge eventually made a good recovery, but remained seriously ill for some time.)

Donovan was detained, the police were called and a murder investigation commenced under the control of Det.Supt Tony Harris, resulting in Donovan being charged with the murder of Lt.Cdr Ian Molyneux and the attempted murder of PO Christopher Brown, CPO David McCoy and Lt.Cdr Christopher Hodge.

Ryan Donovan appeared at Winchester Crown Court on 19 September 2011, pleaded guilty to the murder and attempted murder charges and was sentenced to 25 years imprisonment. He had admitted that the shooting was premeditated.

During the hearing Nigel Lickley QC, prosecuting, said of Cllr Royston Smith and chief executive Alistair Neill, 'There can be no doubt they displayed remarkable courage that day, acting against an armed man. We will not know how many more Donovan would have killed if he had not been stopped.'

It also came to light that the previous year Donovan had told a colleague that he was trying to 'create a massacre in the control room' and the pair had discussed the

computer game 'Grand Auto Theft' in which players took part in a 'shooting frenzy'. Donovan had spent two days drinking in Southampton before the day of the shooting and as he went back to the submarine to start his tour of duty he told another crewmate, 'I am going to kill somebody'. This was taken to be a joke, but sadly proved to be true.

As a result of this tragedy both Cllr Royston Smith and Alistair Neill were awarded the George Medal, the second highest civilian award for gallantry, for their bravery. The highest is the George Cross, awarded posthumously.

They also received a National Police Public Bravery Award in Manchester on 24 May 2012, an award that 'recognises exceptional acts in exceptional circumstances'.

Cllr Royston Smith, GM, and Chief Executive Alistair Neill, GM. (*Courtesy of Southampton City Council*)

ND - #0205 - 270225 - C0 - 234/156/9 - PB - 9781780910857 - Gloss Lamination